STUDIES IN THE U

Deindustrialization

Stephen Bazen and Tony Thirlwall
University of Kent at Canterbury

HEINEMANN
EDUCATIONAL

Heinemann Educational,
a division of Heinemann Educational Books Ltd
Halley Court, Jordan Hill, Oxford OX2 8EJ

OXFORD LONDON EDINBURGH
MELBOURNE SYDNEY AUCKLAND
IBADAN NAIROBI GABORONE HARARE
KINGSTON PORTSMOUTH NH (USA)
SINGAPORE MADRID

First published 1989

British Library Cataloguing in Publication Data
Bazen, Stephen
Deindustrialization.–(Studies in the UK economy)
1. Great Britain. Industries. Decline, history
I. Title II. Thirlwall, A. P. (Anthony Philip) 1941–
III. Series
338.0941

ISBN 0 435 33005 5

Typeset and illustrated by Gecko Limited, Bicester, Oxon
Printed and bound in Great Britain by Biddles Ltd, King's Lynn and Guildford

Acknowledgements

The authors are grateful to Bryan Hurl for his editing of the final version of the book and to Celine Noronha for typing the manuscript.

Thanks are due to the following for permission to reproduce copyright material: *The Age* for the article and cartoon on pp. 87–90; Chapman and Hall for the table on p. 25; *Financial Times* for the articles on pp. 67–69 and 80–81; *Guardian* for the articles on pp. 29–31, 49–51, 77–78; The Controller of Her Majesty's Stationery Office for the table on p. 36 and for the quotes on pp. 81 and 82; National Institute of Economic and Social Research for the tables on pp. 9, 13, 19, 36, 38, 42, 43, 61, 65; Organisation of Economic Cooperation and Development, Paris for the tables on pp. 5 and 16; *The Times* for the article on pp. 53–54 and for the letters on pp. 62–63 and 54–55.

Contents

Preface

The revelation in 1983 that, for the first time since the Industrial Revolution, the United Kingdom's balance of payments in manufactured goods had plunged into deficit – and has worsened every year since – served to spotlight the underlying structural deterioration in the economy which the gains from North Sea oil have since tried to mask. Indeed, the contribution of manufacturing to the GDP (gross domestic product) is now only 22 per cent; three decades ago it was 33 per cent.

As the 1980s have progressed, so the supply side reforms and sustained growth of the GDP have produced claims of a 'Thatcher miracle'. As Professor Thirlwall asked of my own pupils, 'If what has been happening to manufacturing industry and the balance of trade in manufactures is an economic miracle, what then is a disaster?'

The importance of deindustrialization is now being reflected in examination questions. It is a classic example of the dynamic nature of economics that requires the country's two foremost experts on it to provide an up-to-date, authoritative account for A and AS-level study.

Bryan Hurl
Series Editor

Chapter One

Introduction

The subject matter of the phenomenon of deindustrialization is a very important one, and a very topical one in the United Kingdom economy. It affects all our lives, as did the decline in the relative and absolute importance of agriculture in the British economy two centuries ago, and as the shrinkage of the agricultural sector in today's poorer countries in Asia, Africa and Latin America affects the lives of people there. If employment or output in industry declines, this has implications for the overall level of employment and unemployment, for the rate of growth of output (i.e. gross domestic product or GDP), and for the economy's balance of payments position if exports and imports are dominated by industrial goods. All this has further implications for a country's exchange rate (and, therefore, also the rate of inflation), for its rate of interest, and for the whole of economic policy. To study deindustrialization therefore involves a consideration of both micro- and macroeconomic issues.

In the United Kingdom there is a special interest in the phenomenon of deindustrialization because, in comparison with other countries, the process seems to have been the most severe, particularly in terms of the loss of jobs in manufacturing industry and the fall in the share of industrial output in total output. There is an amusing acronymic classification of the countries of the world into HICs (hardly industrialized countries), PICs (partly industrialized countries), NICs (newly industrialized countries), MICs (mature industrialized countries), and DICs (decadent industrialized countries). The United Kingdom is a prime DIC! As our economy apparently moves (without intervention) from being an industrial society to a 'post-industrial' society, there are some very important questions to ask concerning the future of work: whether an economy can sustain itself simply by specialization in service-type activities, and, if not, what is the role of government, and what policies might it pursue, to arrest the decline of industry. This book attempts to address some of the important issues involved.

Chapter Two

What is deindustrialization?

'Deindustrialization has gatecrashed the literature, thereby avoiding the entrance fee of a definition.' F. Blackaby

In 1966, employment in the UK manufacturing sector reached a peak of 9.1 million. Between 1966 and 1987, it fell by 4 million. In the same period, employment in the service sector increased by 3.4 million while total employment fell by 2 million. The contraction of employment was also associated with a stagnant growth of manufacturing output. From 1966 to the oil supply crisis of 1973, manufacturing output increased by 25 per cent, or at an annual growth rate of 3.5 per cent. From 1973 to 1979 (when Mrs Thatcher came to power) manufacturing output fell by 4.1 per cent. Between 1979 and 1982, during the deepest recession since the early 1930s, manufacturing output fell by a further 14 per cent, and only in 1987 did it again reach its 1979 level.

The definition should be cause-free and possess universality

The term deindustrialization refers to a long-term contraction of the manufacturing sector (although some commentators also include mining and quarrying, construction, and gas, electricity and water), but how it should be measured is a source of disagreement. What is needed is an operational definition which gauges the seriousness of the decline of the manufacturing sector. It should also be a **cause-free definition** in the sense that it should not prejudge cause(s). Some definitions of deindustrialization do prejudge the cause(s), rather as the definition of inflation as 'too much money chasing too few goods' prejudges the cause of inflation, and therefore precludes wider analysis.

A further desirable property for an operational definition is that it possesses **universality**. It should be neither time- nor place-specific. It should be easily observable and permit international comparisons.

On this basis we can distinguish between the various definitions that have been suggested. We shall briefly consider two of them.

Singh's definition of deindustrialization

Dr Singh of Cambridge University suggests that deindustrialization occurs when 'the manufacturing sector, without losing price or cost competitiveness, is unable to export enough to pay for the full-employment level of imports'. In other words, deindustrialization *results* from the failure of the manufacturing sector to generate enough foreign exchange in order for the economy to be run at a level of activity corresponding to the full employment of labour.

This is illustrated in Figure 1, which measures imports and exports on the vertical axis and national income on the horizontal axis. Imports are assumed to rise with income, while exports are assumed to be determined by incomes abroad and not by incomes at home. At full employment, planned imports exceed exports, and equilibrium on the balance of payments requires a lower level of income Y_1 which is not sufficient to generate full employment. Jobs in manufacturing (and other activities) are lost.

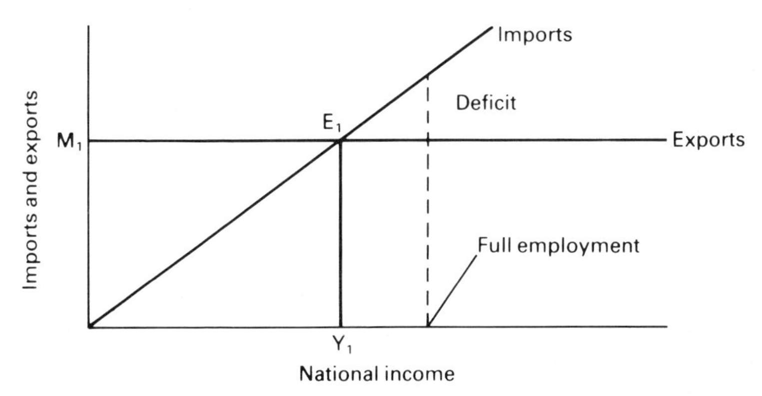

Figure 1 An illustration of Singh's analysis of deindustrialization

It is clear, however, that this definition is not cause-free, since deindustrialization is defined in terms of the trade performance of the manufacturing sector. While, in fact, this may be the most convincing *explanation* of deindustrialization (see later), the cause is still pre-judged and therefore Singh's definition is not satisfactory.

Furthermore, his definition does not possess universality. Most of the non-oil-producing developing countries find it difficult to export enough to pay for all the imports they require for the development process, yet their manufacturing sectors are generally expanding, and therefore these countries are not deindustrializing.

While Singh's view of the causes of deindustrialization in the UK are convincing, his definition of the process is unsatisfactory.

Bacon and Eltis's definition of deindustrialization

Another popular definition was once given by two economists from Oxford University, Bacon and Eltis. They claimed that the excessive growth of resources employed in the non-market sector of the UK economy (consisting mainly of government activities whose outputs are either not marketed or are sold at a loss) had reduced the resources available for the market sector (especially manufacturing), which had consequently contracted. A larger non-market sector had starved the market sector of labour and investment resources which it required to grow.

Deindustrialization is thus defined in terms of the growth of the non-market sector, but again the cause is prejudged. It is possible, in the competition for resources in a fully employed economy, for the growth of one sector to bid resources away from another. On the other hand, in conditions where resources are unemployed or growing, it is quite possible for the non-market sector to be growing while the manufacturing sector is also expanding satisfactorily in terms of employment and output.

The Bacon–Eltis thesis was first put forward with reference to post-war Britain, and then extended to other countries. Subsequent research, however, showed that their explanation of the loss of manufacturing jobs in Britain could not be satisfactorily explained simply by the growth of employment in government service activities (see, for example, Thirlwall 1978).

The two best definitions

The two best definitions of deindustrialization which are cause-free and not time- and place-specific are

- a declining *share* of total employment in manufacturing, and
- an *absolute* decline in employment in manufacturing.

Table 1 (OECD data) shows that most developed economies have experienced a declining share of civilian employment in the manufacturing sector since 1960, and Table 2 (also OECD data) shows a falling share of output in manufacturing relative to GDP. However, this may not reflect an absolute contraction of the manufacturing sector. A falling *share* may simply be the result of employment in manufacturing growing at a slower rate than total employment, and in this sense deindustrialization may not be a cause for concern. A declining share of employment in manufacturing might be expected in the process of development as the composition of demand changes away from manufactured goods towards service-type activities, in-

Table 1 The share of manufacturing in total civilian employment in certain OECD countries

	1960	*1970*	*1979*	*1986*
UK	**36.0**	**34.5**	**29.3**	**22.5**
Canada	23.7	22.3	19.9	17.3
USA	27.1	26.4	22.7	19.1
Japan	21.5	27.0	24.3	24.7
France	27.5	27.8	26.1	22.6
Germany	37.0	39.4	34.3	32.2
Italy	23.0	27.8	26.7	22.9
Netherlands	30.6	26.4	22.3	19.2
Norway	25.3	26.7	20.5	17.2

Table 2 The share of manufacturing in total output in OECD countries

	1960	*1970*	*1979*	*1986*
UK	**32.1**	**28.1**	**24.9**	**21.8**
Canada	23.3	20.4	19.1	17.2*
USA	28.6	25.7	23.8	23.8
Japan	33.9	35.9	30.1	29.3
France	29.1	28.7	27.0	25.6
Germany	40.3	38.2	34.1	33.1
Italy	28.5	28.9	30.6	28.8
Netherlands	33.6	28.2	19.0	19.8
Norway	21.3	21.8	18.2	15.3

* 1984 figure.

cluding leisure pursuits and foreign travel.

On the other hand, an *absolute* decline in manufacturing employment *is* a cause for concern, and this will also mean a declining share of manufacturing employment if employment in other sectors is growing faster, or contracting at a slower rate than employment in manufacturing.

In fact, the only situation in which an absolute decline in employment in manufacturing might provide a misleading picture of the health of the economy is if technology is expanding very rapidly so that labour productivity is also expanding very rapidly, leading to falls in employment. However, as we argue below, technical progress should not be the enemy of employment in the long run since technical progress creates new products, new wants and new manufacturing industries – at least it has done so historically. Technical progress and productivity growth are also vital for countries to remain competitive in the world economy, without which the demand for exports will fall and make employment worse. This consideration gives rise to a distinction in the literature between positive and negative deindustrialization.

Positive and negative deindustrialization

Employment in manufacturing declines when the rate of growth of output is lower than the rate of growth of labour productivity. (Since labour productivity is measured as output per person, it follows that the rate of growth of employment equals the rate of growth of output minus the rate of growth of productivity.) If employment is falling because a high rate of growth of output is being outstripped by an even higher rate of growth of productivity, then it is difficult to regard this decline as a cause for concern. Indeed, it may be thought desirable that the number of hours worked per week, the number of weeks paid holiday and the length of working life should fall secularly as the economy moves into the post-industrial stage. This is **positive deindustrialization.** However, if it is a low growth of output that is being exceeded by a mediocre rate of growth of productivity, then the decline of employment is attributable to a sluggish growth of output and the wealth to finance increased leisure time is not being created. The country is likely to be getting relatively poorer compared with other countries. This is **negative deindustrialization.**

Thus, *positive* deindustrialization occurs when the share of employment in manufacturing falls because of rapid productivity growth, but where displaced labour is absorbed into the non-manufacturing sector. The economy remains at full employment and the GDP per capita is higher. This can be seen by the movement from A to B in Figure 2. On the other hand, *negative* deindustrialization results from a decline in the share of manufacturing in total employment, owing to a slow growth or decline in demand for manufacturing output, and where the labour displaced results in unemployment rather than being absorbed into the non-manufacturing sector. Here the fall in manufacturing employment is associated with stagnation and unemployment. This would be represented by the movement from A to C in Figure 2.

Deindustrialization can therefore be associated with benefits if it is accompanied by fast output growth, or cause severe problems if it is associated with stagnant output. When we come to examine the performance of the manufacturing sector in the UK, we shall see that

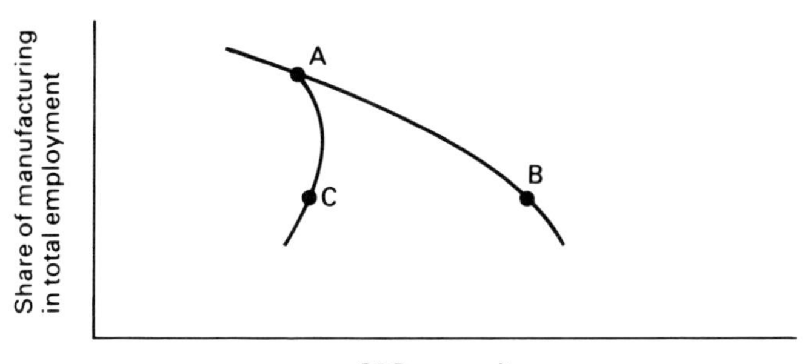

Figure 2 Positive and negative deindustrialization

the deindustrialization experienced has been predominantly of the negative kind.

The definition of deindustrialization we prefer in this book is a long-term absolute decline of employment in the manufacturing sector. This definition is cause-free and permits historical and international comparisons. It also makes clear the significance of deindustrialization for unemployment. If the labour force, defined as all those wishing to work at a particular time, does not decrease in size, a reduction in employment in manufacturing will lead to unemployment unless jobs are created at a fast enough rate elsewhere in the economy – in particular in the service sector.

KEY WORDS

Cause-free definition	**Bacon and Eltis's definition**
Universality	**Positive deindustrialization**
Singh's definition	**Negative deindustrialization**

Reading list

Bacon, R. and Eltis, W., *Britain's Economic Problem: Too Few Producers*, 2nd edn, Macmillan, 1978.

Blackaby, F. (ed), *Deindustrialization*, Heinemann, 1979.

Hare, P.G. and Kirby, M.W., chapter 10 in *An Introduction to British Economic Policy*, Wheatsheaf, 1984.

Rowthorn, R. and Wells, J.R., *Deindustrialisation and Foreign Trade*, Cambridge University Press, 1987.

Singh, A., 'A Third World view', chapter 4 of *Money Talks* (Horrax, H. and McCredie, G., eds), Thames Methuen, 1983.
Thirlwall, A.P., 'The UK's economic problem: a balance of payments constraint', *National Westminster Bank Review*, February 1978.
Thirlwall, A.P., 'Deindustrialization in the UK', *Lloyds Bank Review*, April 1982.

Essay topics

1. What is the major weakness of the Singh definition of deindustrialization?
2. What is the importance of the non-market sector of the economy in the Bacon and Eltis analysis of deindustrialization?
3. Why does the growth of the non-market sector not necessarily imply less resources for manufacturing?
4. What is the difference between positive and negative deindustrialization?

Data Response Question 1

Production in manufacturing industry

The figures in the accompanying table are indexed, 1985 being the base year in which output in all manufacturing sectors is 100 arbitrary units. So, for example, metals the year before (1984) were 6.4 per cent lower in output, and the year after (1986) fell by 0.4 per cent. Study the table and then answer the following questions:

1. Why do all the figures register a fall in 1980 from 1979?
2. Why are chemicals and food, drink and tobacco in 1979 not regarded as typical of the other five sectors of manufacturing?
3. What was the percentage fall in manufacturing output from 1979 to 1981?
4. When did manufacturing return to its 1979 level of output?
5. Is there any real difference between the 1979 and 1988 output for building materials?
6. Have textiles recovered to the 1979 output?
7. Why are these figures a cause for anxiety?

Production in manufacturing industry (Index 1985 = 100)

		Manufacturing	*Metals*	*Building materials*	*Chemicals*	*Engineering and allied*	*Food, drink and tobacco*	*Textiles and clothing*	*Other manufacturing*
1979		105.5	116.8	117.3	93.4	103.6	99.7	115.7	113.0
1980		96.3	88.7	105.7	84.0	96.2	99.0	98.1	101.0
1981		90.6	94.1	94.2	83.5	88.3	97.3	91.0	94.1
1982		90.8	91.5	96.1	83.7	89.3	98.8	89.6	91.7
1983		93.8	93.9	96.6	91.5	92.4	100.0	92.6	93.5
1984		97.7	93.6	100.3	96.9	96.9	100.8	96.0	98.5
1985		*100.0*	*100.0*	*100.0*	*100.0*	*100.0*	*100.0*	*100.0*	*100.0*
1986		100.9	99.6	101.3	102.0	99.3	100.8	100.8	104.6
1987		106.8	108.2	106.6	109.0	104.1	103.4	103.2	115.4
1987	I	102.9	102.8	101.8	105.8	99.6	101.8	101.4	110.6
	II	106.3	108.3	106.2	107.1	103.7	103.4	104.0	114.3
	III	108.3	110.0	108.9	111.2	105.3	103.9	104.3	117.6
	IV	109.8	111.5	109.4	111.9	108.0	104.4	103.2	118.9
1988	I	110.7	117.9	118.0	111.2	106.9	103.7	103.9	123.1
	II	112.8	120.6	114.9	113.1	110.3	106.3	102.0	124.9
	July	115.4	125	119	116	114	106	104	127
	Aug	116.9	125	118	118	117	107	103	127

Source: Statistical Appendix Table 2, *National Institute Economic Review*, No. 126, November 1988.

Chapter Three

The extent of deindustrialization

'*Unless the climate is changed so that steps can be taken to enlarge the manufacturing base, combat import penetration and stimulate the export of manufactured goods, as oil revenues diminish the country will experience adverse effects* [which taken together] *constitute a grave threat to the standard of living . . .*'. Report of House of Lords Select Committee on Overseas Trade

---

In this chapter we discuss deindustrialization as a long-term absolute decline in employment in the manufacturing sector in line with the definition given in the previous chapter.

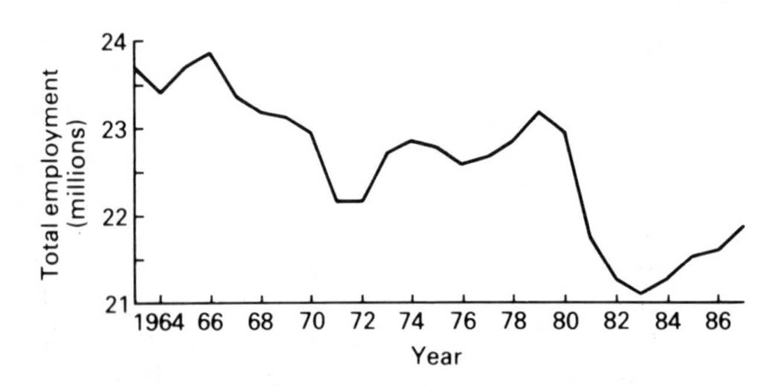

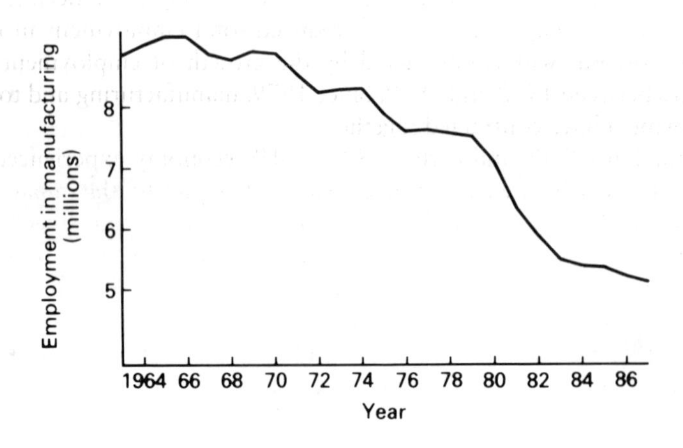

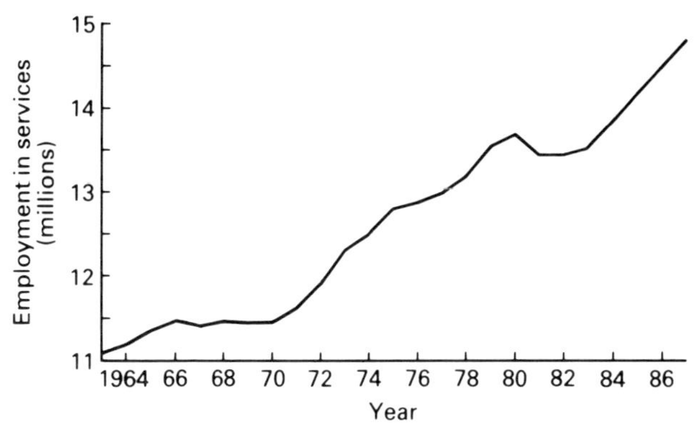

Figure 3 (*see also facing page*) Employment trends between 1963 and 1987

Figure 3 shows the long-term decline of manufacturing employment in the UK, together with trends in employment in the service sector (including Public Administration), and in total employment for the period 1963–87. Since 1966, employment in manufacturing has followed a downward trend with cyclical fluctuations, although since 1977 there has been no upturn. Between 1966 and 1977, nearly 1.9 million jobs were lost in manufacturing, while a further 2.2 million were lost between 1977 and 1987. Employment in services grew rapidly between 1970 and 1980 – some 2.3 million jobs were created – after a period of relatively slow growth during the 1960s. Total employment (excluding the self-employed and the armed forces) fell after 1966 by 0.9 million up to 1972 and thereafter rose slightly, reaching a peak in 1979, and fell dramatically thereafter. Between 1979 and 1987, total employment fell by nearly 1.4 million.

The overall picture, therefore, is one of a long-term decline in manufacturing employment which reduced total employment in the late 1960s, but was counteracted by the growth of employment in services between 1972 and 1979. Since 1979, manufacturing and total employment have contracted together.

In the late 1970s and early 1980s the UK economy experienced a severe **shock** (which we examine in detail in Chapter 6), the impact of which added a large cyclical component to the underlying structural decline. On our definition of deindustrialization, it has been a continuous process since 1966, which was vastly exacerbated by the events of the late 1970s and early 1980s. Between 1979 and 1982, total employment and employment in services both fell, although both have since recovered. Employment in manufacturing, however, has not.

Manufacturing employment by industry

Given the extent of the contraction of manufacturing employment, it is important to see whether it has been the result of the decline of one or two major industries within the manufacturing sector, or whether it has been a widespread phenomenon across all industries.

Table 3 shows changes in the absolute level of employment for industries since the years in which their employment peaked, and for 1966, 1979 and 1982 (the figures are taken from various issues of the *Annual Abstract of Statistics*). The three textile sectors had their peak years in 1951 and experienced a reduction in employment of over 60 per cent up to 1982. Along with the manufacturing sector as a whole, in the majority of industries employment peaked in the 1960s. In three industries – food, drink and tobacco, metal goods, and paper, printing and publishing – the peak years were at the beginning of the 1970s and these have experienced percentage declines lower than the average decline since the peak year.

It is clear, therefore, that although the peak years, and the size of the proportionate decline in employment, vary between industries, all experienced an absolute decline in employment of at least 12 per cent *up to 1979*. Furthermore, in no industry did employment reach its 1979 level by 1982.

Manufacturing employment by region

The maps in Figure 4 show the distribution of manufacturing employment across the eleven **standard regions** of the United Kingdom in 1966, 1979 and 1987. The mass of manufacturing industry and employment is concentrated down a central axis running from the North West, through the West Midlands into the South East of England. These three regions contain over 50 per cent of manufacturing employment. Between 1966 and 1979 when manufacturing employment fell by 1.75 million, or nearly 20 per cent, all regions suffered except the South West and East Anglia. The worst-hit regions were the North West and South East where manufacturing employment fell by 29.1 and 28.8 per cent, respectively.

The typically depressed regions

Between 1979 and 1987, manufacturing employment fell by a further 2.13 million, or nearly 30 per cent. Particularly badly hit during those 'Thatcher years' have been Scotland, Wales, Northern Ireland, the North, North West and Yorkshire and Humberside – the typically depressed regions of the United Kingdom. In all these regions,

Table 3 Employment in UK manufacturing (thousands)

Standard Industrial Classification (1968)	*Peak year*	*Peak-year employment*	*1966*	*1979*	*Change 1966–79 (%)*	*1982*	*Change 1966–82 (%)*
Food, drink and tobacco	1970	891	862	699	−18.9	622	−23
Coal and petroleum products	1961	–	–	35	–	26	–
Chemicals and allied industries	1961	531	527	440	−16.5	390	−26
Metal manufacturing	1961	633	623	449	−27.9	295	−53
Mechanical, instrument and electrical engineering	1966	2377	2377	1803	−24.1	1507	−37
Shipbuilding and marine engineering	1956	581	214	172	−19.7	147	−31
Vehicles	1960	921	853	751	−12.0	559	−34
Metal goods (NES)	1970	640	599	525	−12.4	532	−28
Textiles	1951	1104	811	479	−40.9	314	−61
Leather, leather goods and fur	1951	79	60	39	−35.0	29	−52
Clothing and footwear	1951	698	554	381	−31.2	273	−51
Bricks, pottery, glass and cement	1966	365	365	260	−28.8	211	−42
Timber and furniture	1968	326	319	259	−18.8	206	−35
Paper, printing and publishing	1970	655	651	543	−16.6	498	−23
Other manufacturing industries	1969	367	349	320	−8.3	244	−30
Totals	(1966)	9163	9163	7155	−21.9	5764	−37

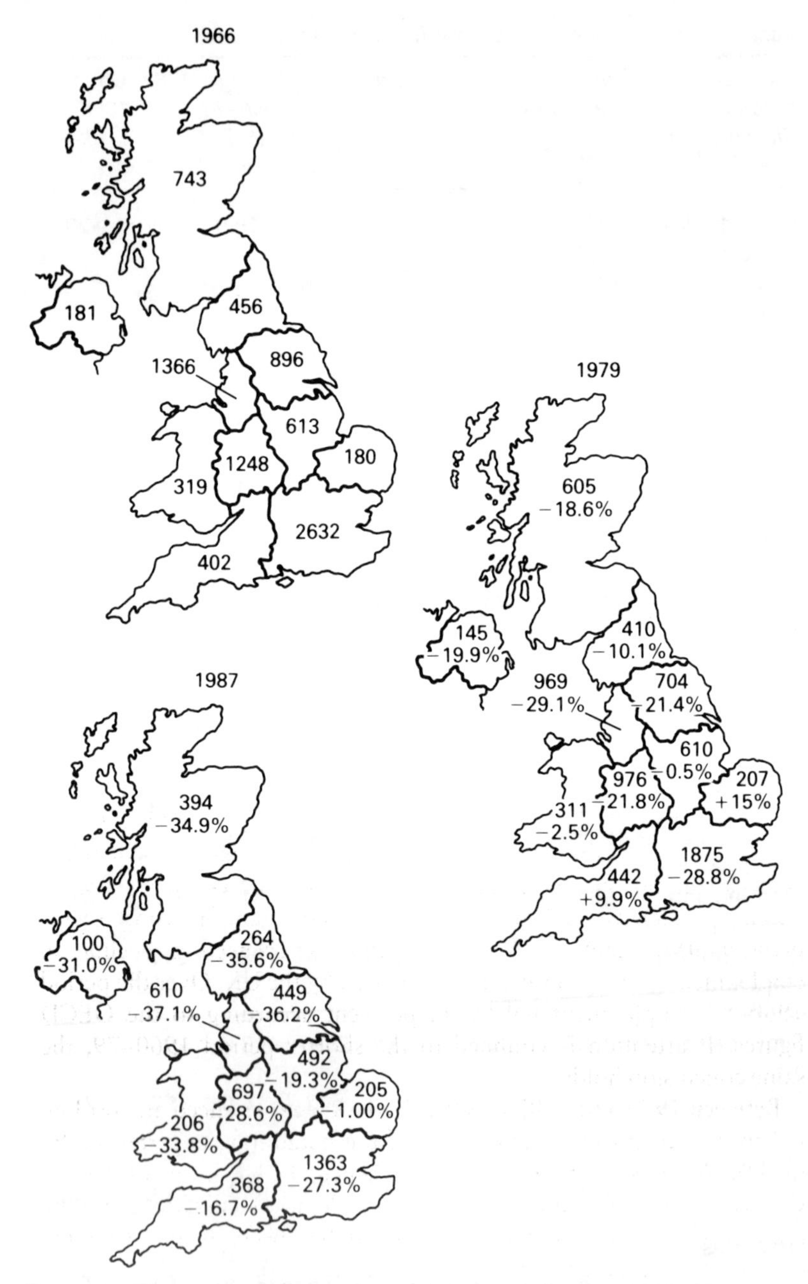

Figure 4 The regional dimension of deindustrialization 1966–87 (shows employment in manufacturing in thousands and the percentage decline)

manufacturing employment has declined by over one-third.

In terms of employment experience, the north-south divide has widened as a result of the economic policies (or lack of them) pursued since 1979. Manufacturing employment has also fallen in the 'south', but not nearly to the same extent, and some of the decline has been offset by much higher employment growth in other sectors – particularly in services and construction – which has prevented unemployment from rising as fast as in the 'north'.

Regional disparities in employment growth and unemployment do, of course, have welfare implications; but they can also affect adversely the functioning of the total economy. For example, demand pressure in the 'south' can affect wage inflation, the price of land and house prices, the effects of which 'spill over' into other regions causing a higher level of aggregate inflation for any given level of aggregate demand in the economy as a whole. Thus regional disparities can worsen the conflict between macroeconomic objectives. Only an active regional policy which discriminates in favour of depressed regions, as far as the location of economic activity is concerned, can cope with these problems of regional imbalance.

Britain compared with other industrialized countries

If employment in manufacturing in the rest of the industrialized world has declined over a long period, the process of deindustrialization in the UK might simply be considered as part of a decreasingly important role played by manufacturing activities in the world economy at large.

However, as Table 4 shows, of the 23 countries for which the comparison can be made, the majority of OECD countries experienced an *increase* in employment in their manufacturing sector between 1960 and 1986. No country experienced a decline in employment of the proportion experienced by the UK. Over the period 1960–87, employment fell by 42 per cent according to the OECD figures. If attention is confined to the shorter period 1960–79, the same conclusion holds.

Between 1979 and 1987 no OECD country experienced an absolute fall in manufacturing employment of the magnitude experienced by the UK. Although not alone in its experience, the UK is one of the few OECD countries to experience significant deindustrialization, and the reduction in manufacturing employment has been by far the most extensive in the UK since 1979.

Table 4 Manufacturing employment in OECD countries 1960–86* (thousands)

	1960	*1979*	*Change 1960–79 (%)*	*1986*	*Change 1960–86 (%)*
Canada	1 406†	2 047	+45.6	1985	+41.2
USA	16 796	21 040	+25.3	18 994	+13.1
Japan	7 990	11 070	+38.5	12 290	+53.8
Australia	1 111	1 177	+5.9	1 061	−4.5
Austria	858	(850)	−1.0	876	+2.1
Belgium	1 043	888	−14.9	741	−29.0
Denmark‡	741	793	+7.0	742	+0.1
Finland	431	582	+35.0	532	+23.4
France	6 322	5 291	−16.3	4 506	−28.7
Germany	(9 433)§	(8 370)	−11.3	7 723	−18.1
Greece‡	598	994	+66.2	1 012	+69.2
Iceland‡	24	38	+58.3	42‖	+75.0
Ireland	168†	(228)	+35.7	200	+19.1
Italy¶	3 735	4 716	+26.3	4 038	+8.1
Luxemburg¶	53	58	+9.4	52	−1.9
Netherlands	1 082	(1037)	−4.2	959	−11.4
Norway	331	370	+11.8	346	+4.5
Portugal	571	(865)	+51.5	919	+60.9
Spain	2 009	2 742	+36.5	2 166	+7.8
Sweden‡	1 499	1 359	−9.3	(1 287)	−14.1
Switzerland‡	1 227	1 229	+0.1	1 213	−1.1
Turkey	885	1 572	+77.6	1 904	+115.1
UK	**8 996**	**7 253**	**−19.3**	**5 243**	**−41.7**

Figures in brackets are not strictly comparable with previous years.
* Wage and salary earners in the manufacturing sector unless otherwise specified. † 1961. ‡ Civilian employment in industry. § 1962. ‖ 1983. ¶ Wage and salary earners in industry.

KEY WORDS

Shock
Standard regions
North–south divide

Reading list

Armstrong, H. and Taylor, J., *Regional Policy and the North–South Divide*, Employment Institute, 1988.

Turner, P. and McCormick, B., 'The north–south divide', *Economic Review*, vol. 5, Sept. 1987.

Essay topics

1. Describe the pattern of employment change in manufacturing and services since 1963.
2. What problems are caused by regional economic imbalances in an economy?
3. How has the manufacturing sector in Britain fared compared with other industrialized countries?

Data Response Question 2

Manufacturing employment in OECD countries

Re-examine Table 4 in this chapter. It is clear that some countries have experienced an absolute decline in manufacturing employment, while others have experienced an increase. Can you think of any characteristics which distinguish the two sets of countries?

Chapter Four

Does deindustrialization matter?

If manufacturing industry contracts, there is a real danger that the whole economy will stagnate . . .

Having documented the decline of employment in the UK manufacturing sector by industry and by region, and seeing that it has generally been more pronounced than in other industrialized countries, it is now important that we consider the question of whether deindustrialization matters.

In this chapter we outline three important reasons why a strong manufacturing sector is both necessary and desirable for the overall health of the UK economy.

- Firstly, there are the obvious implications for unemployment.
- Secondly, it is widely recognized that the manufacturing sector has certain unique growth-inducing characteristics not found in other sectors of the economy.
- Thirdly, we emphasize the importance of manufacturing industry for a healthy balance of payments, and hence for the *growth* of the economy if it is not to be constrained by balance of payments deficits.

Historically, and up to as recently as 1982, Britain always had a surplus of trade in manufactured goods, which helped to pay for imports of food, raw materials and fuel; but now this is no longer true. If the economy is to grow faster and unemployment is to be substantially reduced, the performance of the UK manufacturing sector is of vital importance. If manufacturing industry contracts, there is a real danger that the whole economy will stagnate through a lack of technological dynamism and severe balance of payments constraints on growth.

Unemployment

Deindustrialization will lead to **unemployment** if the growth of employment elsewhere in the economy is insufficient to absorb the labour shed by the manufacturing sector (unless the size of the workforce declines).

Since 1966 deindustrialization has led to higher unemployment in the UK (see Table 5, the figures in which are taken from various issues of the *Annual Abstract of Statistics*). Agriculture and production industries other than manufacturing shed over 800 000 jobs between 1966 and 1979, while over two million jobs were lost in manufacturing itself. The increase in jobs created by the service sector was insufficient to absorb the loss of jobs in manufacturing – so that, together with the increase in the size of the labour force, unemployment rose by over one million. Then, between 1979 and 1983, employment fell in all of the sectors listed; manufacturing in particular lost 1.7 million jobs while unemployment rose by a similar number.

Since 1983, total employment has increased by virtue of a pronounced rise in employment in the service sector. Deindustrialization has therefore been responsible for much of the high unemployment that the UK has experienced since 1966.

Table 5 Changes in employment 1966–87 (thousands)

	*1966–79**	*1979–83†*	*1983–87*
Change in labour force	+154	+241	+1600
Change in total employment‡	−959	−2106	+750
Change in unemployment§	+1063	+1640	−80
Change in employment in:			
Agriculture	−110	−30	−29
Manufacturing	−2008	−1728	−380
Other production industries	−706	−268	−187
Services	+865	−81	+1344
Change in self-employment and armed forces	+90	+343	+637

* Based on SIC 1968 classification. † Based on SIC 1980 classification. ‡ Excluding the self-employed and armed forces. § Excluding school-leavers.

Growth

A related, though conceptually distinct, worry about deindustrialization concerns the role that the manufacturing sector plays in the process of **economic growth**. It is often asserted that the manufacturing sector is the 'engine of growth', for reasons summed up in what have become known as **Kaldor's Growth Laws** (after Professor Nicholas Kaldor, the Cambridge economist).

There are three laws to consider. The first law states that there is a strong positive relationship between the growth of manufacturing industry and the growth rate of the economy as a whole in a *causal* sense – and not simply because manufacturing activity constitutes a large fraction of the **gross domestic product** (GDP). The second and third laws are concerned with accounting for this strong positive relationship.

The second law states that there is a strong positive relationship between the growth of manufacturing output and the rate of growth of productivity in manufacturing.

The third law states that there is a strong positive relationship between the rate at which manufacturing output and employment grows and the rate at which productivity grows outside manufacturing, because resources are used which would otherwise be unemployed or have a lower productivity.

The first growth law

Professor Kaldor, in his analysis of growth-rate differences between twelve OECD countries, found a strong correlation between the growth of manufacturing output and the growth of the GDP; and the faster the growth of manufacturing *relative* to the growth of the GDP, the faster the growth of national income. In other words, what distinguishes fast-growing countries from slow-growing countries is whether the *share* of manufacturing output in total output is increasing or not.

Since growth-rate differences between countries are largely accounted for by differences in productivity growth (that is, differences in the growth of output per person), rather than differences in the growth of the labour force, Kaldor concluded that there must be a relationship between the rate at which manufacturing output grows and the rate at which productivity grows inside and outside manufacturing. This was also confirmed by his research, and has been supported by other research. This leads to the second and third laws.

The second growth law

As far as productivity growth in manufacturing is concerned, Kaldor found that, on average, a 1 per cent growth of output leads to a 0.5 per cent increase in productivity growth. This relationship (the second law) arises from the existence of increasing returns to scale in the manufacturing sector, both static and dynamic.

Static increasing returns to scale means that if *all* inputs are increased, output rises by more than in proportion to the increase in inputs, leading to an increase in output per person. **Dynamic increasing returns** relate largely to technical progress embodied in capital goods, which means that the faster the rate of capital accumulation associated with output growth, the faster the rate of growth of labour productivity. An increase in the rate of growth of output therefore leads to a cumulative expansion via increased productivity.

These characteristics do not appear to be found in sectors other than manufacturing.

This second law is also sometimes known as *Verdoorn's Law*, after the Dutch economist P.J. Verdoorn who first mooted the relationship in 1949.

The third growth law

As far as productivity growth *outside* manufacturing is concerned, Kaldor found a strong negative relationship between productivity growth in the economy as a whole and employment growth outside manufacturing (holding employment growth in manufacturing constant), therefore indicating that fast employment growth in non-manufacturing activities slows up overall productivity growth, and vice versa. This is because, very often, there is only a very loose relationship between output and employment in sectors like agriculture, retailing and other service activities, so that when employment rises or falls, output hardly changes at all. This phenomenon is often referred to as **disguised unemployment.**

Disguised unemployment is very prevalent in the agricultural sector of Third World countries and in the petty service trades found in the urban areas; but it is a phenomenon also found in more industrialized economies.

Many activities outside manufacturing are also subject to **diminishing returns**, so that if the labour force is reduced, the marginal product of labour, and the overall level of productivity, rises.

The cumulative effect

Taken together, these three laws mean that a country which obtains an initial advantage in productive activities that have favourable growth characteristics will tend to sustain that advantage by exploiting increasing returns to scale, both static and dynamic, leading to higher productivity and competitiveness.

For example, a favourable shock which increases the rate of growth of output in manufacturing will lead to faster productivity growth, which in turn, by making goods more competitive, expands the demand for output, which again induces productivity growth, and so on. This is sometimes called a **virtuous circle of growth**. If, as we have observed in the UK since 1966, the rate of growth of manufacturing output has been stagnant or it declines, the opposite occurs, creating a **vicious circle** of low economic growth, low productivity growth, deteriorating competitiveness and the shedding of labour from the manufacturing sector owing to a lack of domestic and foreign demand for the products.

The balance of payments

While the foregoing laws can explain differences in the growth experience of countries, the initial impetus to the growth of manufacturing output is not determined. Historically, the stimulus has come from the agricultural sector in the early stages of development and from exports in the later stages.

One of the major reasons why Britain was the first country to industrialize was that it experienced an early agricultural revolution which raised productivity in agriculture and increased the demand for manufactured goods as inputs and as finished products. But Britain did not choose to specialize in agriculture, nor is it rich in raw materials. The lack of self-sufficiency in food and the paucity of raw materials leads us on to the third reason why deindustrialization matters, namely the **balance of payments.**

The UK needs to import foodstuffs and raw materials, and to pay for these (in order to maintain equilibrium on the balance of payments current account) the UK exports mainly manufactured goods, various services ('invisibles'), and more recently North Sea oil. North Sea oil production has already begun to level off and will generate lower export earnings in the future (unless the dollar price of oil rises by more than in proportion to the fall in output), which will increasingly leave exports of services and manufactured goods to pay for the necessary imports of food and raw materials (including oil in the future).

Traditionally, the balance of trade in goods (the **visible balance**) has been in deficit, although exports of manufactured goods used to exceed imports of manufactures. The latter is now no longer true. Since 1983 the balance of trade in manufactured goods has been in deficit, and the trend appears to be deteriorating. This means that only a surplus of trade in services (the **invisible balance**) is left to pay for food, raw material requirements and the appetite for foreign manufactured goods. This is not a sustainable situation, and without any improvement in the manufacturing trade balance, the growth of the whole economy will have to be slowed up to cut back imports.

This leads us to the important concept of balance of payments **constrained growth**, and the measurement of a country's balance of payments **equilibrium growth rate.**

Balance of payments equilibrium growth rate

Theory

For the current account of the balance of payments to balancc, the value of exported goods and services must equal the value of imported goods and services. For an equilibrium to be preserved, the *rates of growth* of the values of exports and imports must be equal.

Elasticity

How fast the value of exports grows depends firstly on how fast export prices are growing; and secondly on how fast the demand for exports is growing which will depend partly on price competitiveness and partly on how fast world trade (or income) is growing.

The relationship between two growth rates is in economics called an **elasticity**; that is, an elasticity is the percentage change in one variable divided by the percentage change in another. Thus the relationship between the growth of exports and the growth rate of relative prices of home and foreign goods is called the *price elasticity of demand for exports*, and the relationship between the growth of exports and the growth of world income is called the *income elasticity of demand for exports*.

Likewise for imports. How fast the value of imports grows depends firstly on how fast import prices are growing; and secondly on how fast the demand for imports is growing, which will depend partly on how competitive imports are and partly on how fast income (or more accurately, expenditure) is growing within the country. The relationship between import growth and relative price changes is called the *price elasticity of demand for imports*, and the relationship between the growth of imports and the growth of domestic income is called the *income elasticity of demand for imports*.

If we make the assumption that in the long run there is very little change in the relative prices of exports and imports (measured in a common currency), then the growth of imports and exports is dominated by income changes at home and abroad. There will be a certain growth of domestic income which just keeps the growth of imports in line with the growth of exports. That growth of income consistent with balance of payments equilibrium on current account will equal the rate of growth of export volume divided by the income elasticity of demand for imports. This defines, a country's *balance of payments constrained growth rate*, and is illustrated in Figure 5.

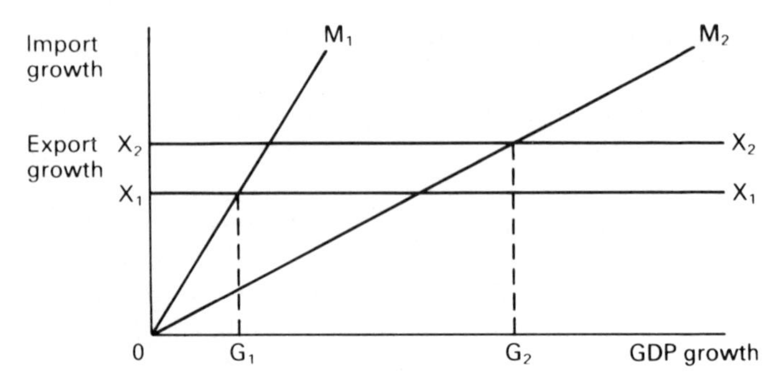

Figure 5 A country's balance of payments constrained growth rate

X_1 and X_2 show different levels of export *growth*. Lines OM_1 and OM_2 show the relationship between import growth and GDP growth, so that the slope of the curve measures the *income elasticity of demand for imports*. The steeper the curve the higher the income elasticity. Where X and M lines cross, this defines the GDP growth rate consistent with balance of payments equilibrium. It can be immediately seen that a country with a low export growth (X_1) and a high income elasticity of demand for imports (M_1) will have a lower growth rate (G_1) than a country with a higher growth of exports (X_2) and a lower income elasticity of demand for imports (M_2), whose growth rate will be G_2.

Empirical Evidence

There is a lot of empirical evidence for the advanced industrialized countries that the actual experience of countries is very close to the growth rate predicted by the above model. That is, no country can grow for very long faster than the rate of growth consistent with balance of payments equilibrium on current account, because there is a limit to the ability and willingness to finance deficits.

Tables 6 and 7 give some evidence for a variety of countries over different time periods of fitting the foregoing analysis to data on export growth and the income elasticity of demand for imports, for comparison of the estimated growth with the actual growth experience. It will be noticed that the UK is estimated to have one of the lowest growth rates consistent with balance of payments equilibrium because its export record is so poor, and also has the worst growth record of any industrialized country. Japan, by contrast, has the highest balance of payments equilibrium growth rate, and has also experienced the fastest rate of growth, while at the same time running balance of payments surpluses because it has not been growing as fast

Table 6 Actual and equilibrium growth rates 1953–76

	Change in real GDP (%)	*Change in export volume (%)*	*Income elasticity of demand for imports*	*Balance of payments equilibrium growth rate**
UK	**2.71**	**4.46**	**1.51**	**2.95**
France	4.95	8.78	1.62	5.42
Germany	4.96	9.99	1.89	5.29
Italy	4.96	12.09	2.25	5.37
Belgium	4.07	9.24	1.94	4.76
Netherlands	4.99	9.38	1.82	5.15
Denmark	3.58	6.77	1.31	5.17
Sweden	3.67	7.16	1.76	4.07
Canada	4.81	6.02	1.20	5.02
USA	3.23	5.88	1.51	3.89
Japan	8.55	16.18	1.23	13.15

* The second column divided by the third column.
Source: Thirlwall (1986).

Table 7 Actual and equilibrium growth rates 1970–85

	Change in real GDP (%)	*Change in exports (%)*	*Income elasticity of demand for imports*	*Balance of payments equilibrium growth rate**
UK	**1.9**	**4.7**	**2.14**	**2.2**
France	3.5	6.3	2.42	2.6
Germany	2.4	5.0	1.92	2.6
Italy	2.6	5.2	2.83	1.8
Belgium	2.7	5.0	2.64	1.9
Netherlands	2.2	4.3	2.00	2.4
Norway	3.9	4.4	1.43	3.1
Sweden	2.2	3.8	2.53	1.5
Canada	3.4	5.0	1.70	2.8
USA	2.5	5.7	2.32	2.5

* The second column divided by the third column.
Source: Bairam (1988).

as it could without going into balance of payments deficit.

From the point of view of economic recovery in the UK, any programme that aims to increase economic growth, other than one based on trade, will soon run into a balance of payments constraint. If the UK economy is going to experience job-creating growth, either exports must grow more rapidly or measures must be implemented to reduce the income elasticity of demand for imports. We return to these issues in Chapter 7.

Export of services

The model outlined above is based upon equilibrium on the current account of the balance of payments, so that a higher rate of growth of **exports of services** would serve as well as exports of manufactured goods. However, there are important reasons why the potential growth in exports of services may be limited in a way that the growth in exports of manufactured goods is not.

Firstly, as recently suggested by the House of Lords Committee on Overseas Trade (consult the reading list), trade in services is limited in the sense that only a small proportion of services is tradeable (perhaps 20 per cent). A recent study by economists at the Bank of England pointed out that in 1979 the UK service sector exported only 11 per cent of its gross output (compared with 33 per cent in manufacturing).

Secondly, looking at the actual behaviour of service exports, the period 1975–84 saw a 5 per cent growth in volume compared with a 21 per cent growth in manufacturing exports. Moreover, throughout this period, the value of exports of manufactured goods has always been more than twice the value of service exports, with no apparent tendency for this differential to narrow.

Thirdly, in both services and manufacturing, the UK's share of world exports has fallen. Between 1968 and 1983 the share of manufactured exports fell from 9.6 to 6.2 per cent while the share of world exports of services fell more noticeably from 11.9 to 7.3 per cent. While it is clear that exports of services do make an important contribution to the current account, it is unlikely that the growth of exports necessary to *raise* the rate of growth of output consistent with balance of payments equilibrium can be provided by the service sector. Exports of manufactured goods are more important in terms of their contribution to the value of total UK exports and in terms of growth, both actual and potential. This contribution will become increasingly important as earnings from oil exports decline over the next twenty years.

KEY WORDS

Unemployment
Economic growth
Kaldor's Growth Laws
Gross domestic product
Static increasing returns to scale
Dynamic increasing returns
Disguised unemployment
Diminishing returns
Virtuous circle of growth
Vicious circle
Balance of payments
Visible balance
Invisible balance
Constrained growth
Equilibrium growth rate
Elasticity
Exports of services

Reading list

Lord Aldington, 'Britain's manufacturing industry', *Royal Bank of Scotland Review*, Sept. 1986.

Bairam, E., 'Balance of payments, the Harrod foreign trade multiplier and economic growth: the European and North American experience 1970–85', *Applied Economics*, Dec. 1988.

House of Lords, *Report of the Select Committee on Overseas Trade*, HMSO, 1985 (summarized in *Economic Review*, Jan. 1986).

Kaldor, N., *Causes of the Slow Rate of Growth of the United Kingdom Economy*, Cambridge University Press, 1966.

McCombie, J.S.L., 'Kaldor's laws in retrospect', *Journal of Post-Keynesian Economics*, Spring 1983.

Thirlwall, A.P., 'Deindustrialization in the United Kingdom', *Lloyds Bank Review*, April 1982.

Thirlwall, A.P., *Balance of Payments Theory and the United Kingdom Experience*, 3rd edn, chapter 10, Macmillan, 1986.

Essay topics

1. What are the implications of deindustrialization for the level of unemployment in the economy?
2. Why is manufacturing industry sometimes referred to as 'the engine of growth'?
3. In what ways does manufacturing output growth induce productivity growth in manufacturing?
4. Why does productivity tend to increase outside manufacturing when manufacturing industry absorbs more resources from other sectors?

5. In what way does the decline in the trade balance in manufactures constrain the growth rate of the whole economy?
6. What determines a country's balance of payments equilibrium growth rate, and why is the rate so low for the UK?

Data Response Question 3

Britain's share of manufactured exports

Read the accompanying article from the *Guardian* of 17 October 1985 (the House of Lords report referred to is mentioned in our reading list), and then answer the following questions.

1. Why is the deficit on the balance of trade unlikely to self-correct?
2. What kind of indirect effect would the failure of the trading sector have on non-trading sectors of the economy?
3. Why will it be difficult for the service sector to offset the decline of North Sea oil and manufactured trade in the UK balance of payments?
4. What factors caused the decline of price competitiveness between 1977 and 1980?
5. Why is the control of inflation in the short term likely to lead to 'the long-term erosion of the position of our traders, especially manufacturers'?
6. What kind of 'microeconomic measures' could be implemented to improve Britain's trade performance?
7. Do you agree with the author's conclusion that the future is bleak?

Sans oil, sans trade, sans everything . . .

THE DAMNING report from the House of Lords select committee on trade cannot be dismissed as lightly as the government pretends. It is a weighty and carefully argued document which amply substantiates its conclusion that our trade prospects "constitute a grave threat to the standard of living of the British people. Failure to recognise these dangers now could have a devastating effect on the future economic and political stability of the nation."

Nor can one seriously cavil with the view that the problem is not self-correcting, as the government claims. We have had, through much of our industrial history, long experience of laissez faire, and they were years in which Britain's relative economic decline proceeded apace.

The success stories of the post-war era – West Germany, Japan and France – have never bilked at subsidy or intervention where the need was carefully established by clear market failure.

Our trading sectors are crucial to the performance of the economy as a whole. Not only is trade capable of directly generating jobs in export industries or import-competing businesses, but its success or failure has powerful indirect effects on every other part of the economy, regardless of whether they are themselves involved in foreign trade or not.

If exports grow slowly – either because of depressed foreign markets or a falling share of those markets – then imports must also grow slowly. This can be achieved in theory by a fall in the currency, which makes exports cheaper in foreign markets and foreigners' exports to us more expensive in pounds.

But that fall in the exchange rate works to improve trading performance only by pushing up import prices and hence inflation. So in order to stem the inflationary effects, British governments have repeatedly slammed on the economic brakes. Imports are then controlled not by price changes, but by demand changes. Tax increases or spending cuts, of course, affect everyone in the economy, including services.

The reason why manufacturing is in turn crucial is simply because of its disproportionate importance in our foreign trade. Though forming only 25 per cent of total national output, it still earns 40 per cent of all our foreign exchange.

Indeed, the Lords report points out that a 3 per cent rise in service exports is required merely to offset a 1 per cent drop in manufacturing exports. And that is extremely unlikely, since services have anyway seen their share of world markets drop even more sharply than manufactures.

Manufacturing has to be put back squarely at the centre of policy-making concern, if only because the present performance of our non-oil trade implies the most devastating black hole in the balance of payments as soon as North Sea oil even stops increasing its contribution to exports, let alone actually begins to decline.

That black hole can only be filled, unless policy is changed quickly, by an inflationary fall in the pound or by a deflationary tightening of interest rate and budget policy which will put paid to the hopes that unemployment can come down. Without oil, we would have had a serious exchange rate crisis several years ago. As oil stops growing, the prospect of crisis can only come closer.

The deterioration in our manufacturing performance has, of course, been going on for many years, and has many chronic causes, including cultural attitudes, poor management,

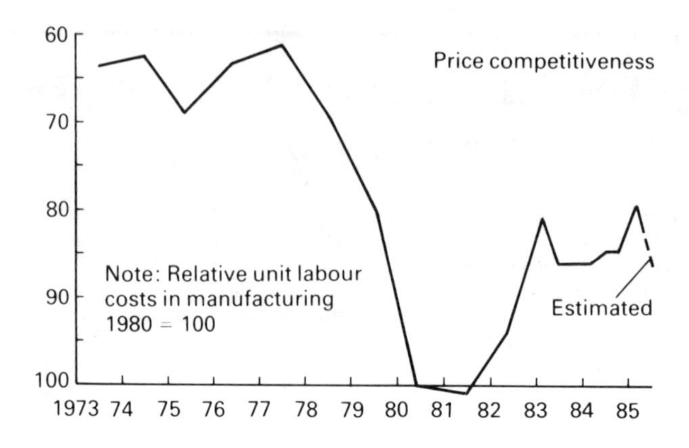

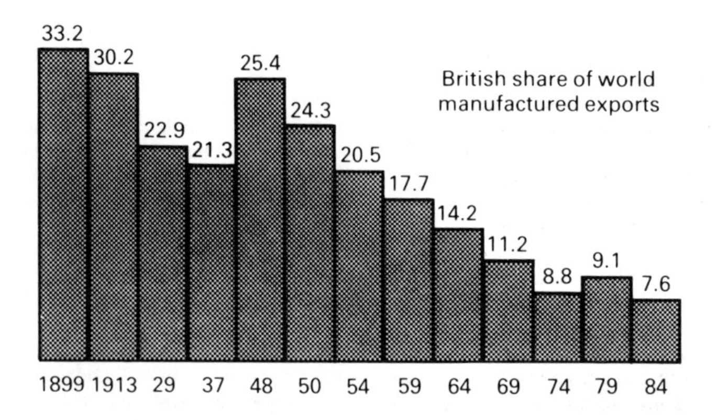

conservative bankers, an inadequately trained work force, and low levels and efficiency of investment. But governments have not helped.

This government is particularly responsible for the collapse in manufacturing trade performance since 1979. Through the seventies, Britain's share of world manufacturing markets actually managed to stabilise for the first time in a century, in part due to the stability of price competitiveness shown in the top graph.

If Britain's costs went up more than those abroad (mainly due to wage increases), the government offset the adverse effects on price competitiveness by allowing a fall in the pound to compensate. That policy was abandoned when sterling was "uncapped" in 1977, and then thrown sharply into reverse by the incoming Tory government in 1979.

Despite a sharp acceleration in wage increases due in part to the aftermath of Labour's incomes policies and in part to the government's doubling of VAT, the Chancellor allowed sterling to rise thus compounding the loss of price competitiveness which reached a scale never before recorded in IMF statistics.

It should be no surprise that the interval of stable world market shares during the seventies has given way to falling market shares in manufactures. Outlets abroad were closed for good. Manufacturers which went to the wall in that terrible period in which their output dropped

by a fifth will not be brought back to life easily.

At least, though, it seemed until this year that the government had learned from its mistakes, even if it could not undo them. Treasury ministers allowed the pound to shift gently downwards to recoup much of the lost price competitiveness, as the graph shows. Since the early spring, however, the pound has once again bounced back.

Once again, the government's motive was the control of inflation. And once again, the cost of that temporary gain is likely to be the long-term erosion of the position of our traders, especially manufacturers. On Bank of England estimates, the rise in the pound in the second quarter alone caused a loss of price competitiveness of 9 per cent.

The Lords report contains a plethora of sensible recommendations. Much of the problem of British trade performance – which has contributed more than anything else to the phenomenon of slow growth and the "British disease" – can only be dealt with by micro-economic measures.

It is surely essential too that there is a broad tripartisan approach to supporting manufacturing, which has been one of the victims of Britain's political process. There is as yet no common sense of national purpose about helping our trading sectors, which is perhaps the sharpest contrast with the Japanese, French and Germans.

Banks need to be persuaded to lend to industry on the basis of market opportunities, rather than the liquidation value of the proposed plant and machinery, which may be minimal in high technology and specific processes. More graduates need to go into industry, and they need to have industrial skills.

The government can also do much by applying the lessons of some of its most successful intervention – notably the extension services to spread good technological practice in agriculture – to small manufacturing businesses. Quality circles and statistical process control are prime examples of techniques with wide application.

Only the government can improve the standard of training, when the individual interest of each firm is to cut spending which would benefit everyone in order to rely on other firms' trained manpower. The skills gap yawns widest at intermediate level, and is most responsible for low British productivity even when the same capital equipment is being used as abroad.

The Treasury must also stop taking macro-economic measures which bear most heavily on our trading sectors (through an overvalued exchange rate) and on investment (through high interest rates). One alternative is not to deflate, and to tackle the root problem of high wage increases from core groups of the employed. Another is to deflate through tax rises and spending cuts which hit the whole economy.

The disaster of the Thatcher years is that none of these micro- or macro-economic paths have been followed. All ministers serve up is some mystical appeal to changing attitudes. The sad truth is that since 1979 we have bought a temporary relief to inflation at the cost of long-term damage to our trading sectors and economic performance. Our future, as the oil stops growing, is indeed bleak.

Christopher Huhne
Economics Correspondent

Chapter Five

The causes of deindustrialization since 1966

There are factors that make the income elasticity of demand for UK exports of manufactured goods low, and the income elasticity of imports high.

There have been four main views put forward to explain the process of deindustrialization:

- technical progress
- the Bacon–Eltis thesis
- the impact of North Sea oil, and
- the weak trade performance of the UK manufacturing sector.

Each of them purports to explain the long-term decline in manufacturing employment. In assessing these views, we shall also look at wider evidence to check their consistency.

Technical progress

Technical progress is claimed to have led to capital displacing labour in the production process. We know from the concept of the **production function**, which relates output to inputs, that labour and capital are used together to produce output. In explaining deindustrialization, it is claimed that technical progress has been of a labour-saving nature.

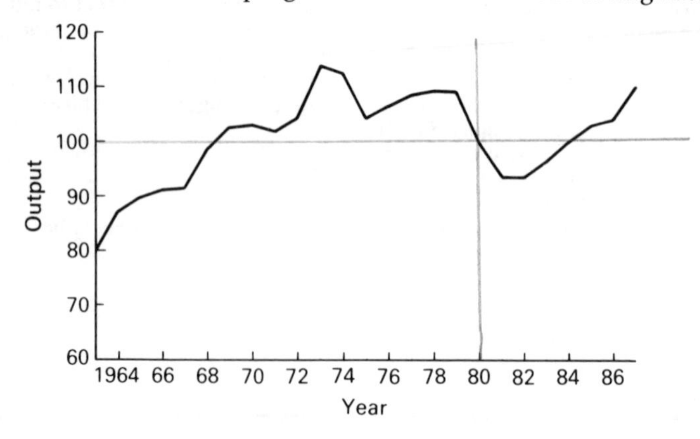

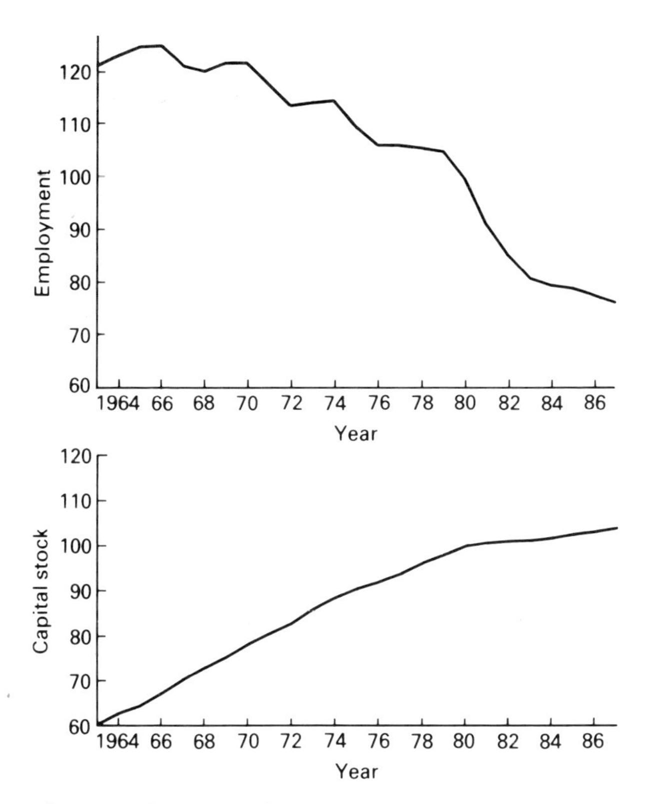

Figure 6 (*see also facing page*) Trends in employment, output and capital between 1963 and 1987 (indexed to 1980 = 100)

In Figure 6 we have plotted trends for the capital stock, employment and output in manufacturing for the period 1963–87. It is clear that the capital stock has grown fairly smoothly while the trend in employment is downwards, although with cyclical variations. Manufacturing output also follows a cyclical pattern, but was growing up to 1973 and falling thereafter.

Since the capital stock is fixed in the short run, it is employment that adjusts to cyclical fluctuations in output. However, it is not possible to conclude that technical progress was labour-saving merely because the capital stock was growing while employment in manufacturing was falling secularly. As the price of labour rises relative to the price of capital, there will always tend to be a substitution process going on. Having said this, it is almost certainly the case that in certain industries within manufacturing, increased mechanization resulting from technical progress will have displaced labour.

But one must distinguish clearly the *microeconomic* consequences of technical progress from the *macroeconomic* consequences. There is no reason why, at the aggregate level, technical progress should mean *less* manufacturing employment. Technical progress involves process innovation or product innovation or both. **Process innovation** at a given level of output, involving capital in new ways of producing things, will lead to the displacement of labour, but at the same time will involve more investment which increases aggregate demand (and therefore employment). **Product innovation** at a given level of output may or may not displace labour. New products and more competitive products increase demand and therefore can create more employment.

Examples of employment-creating product innovations are the washing machine, motor vehicle and aeroplane; while the microchip, which has permitted increased mechanization, has also created micro-computers and pocket calculators and has improved existing products over a wide spectrum.

Historically, technical progress has created more jobs than it has destroyed at the aggregate level. A study in 1985 of the causes of unemployment, by Professors Layard and Nickell at the London School of Economics, found little evidence that technology embodied in the capital stock was limiting employment.

Finally, it is important to point out that even in the most technologically advanced countries, such as Japan, manufacturing employment has been growing.

Contrary to the view that technical progress is the cause of deindustrialization in the United Kindom, the opposite argument could be put that it is because technical change has been *sluggish* in the UK that demand has shifted away from UK goods towards foreign-produced goods whose price competitiveness, reliability and quality have been improved by innovation.

While no quantitative conclusions are possible, it is our view that technical progress cannot be responsible for the shedding of four million jobs in UK manufacturing between 1966 and 1987.

The Bacon and Eltis thesis

A more detailed account of deindustrialization has been offered by the Oxford economists, Bacon and Eltis, in a controversial book published in 1976 entitled *Britain's Economic Problem: Too Few Producers*. On the basis of a wealth of evidence, they claim that the increased proportion of resources devoted to those public sector activities that do not market their output (including loss-making nationalized industries) has *crowded out* resources available to the manufacturing and other sectors that do market their output.

Their thesis can be illustrated in various ways using the national income accounts. *National income from the expenditure side* is equal to the sum of consumption, investment and the balance of payments surplus (exports minus imports). The balance of payments surplus, by definition, is made up of **marketable output**, but consumption and investment may either be in the marketable output or **non-marketable output** sectors. It follows that if there is an increase in the amount of expenditure devoted to non-marketable output, and the consumption of marketable output does not fall, then investment in the marketable output sector and/or the balance of payments must suffer. Or in terms of shares of national income, if the share of expenditure in the non-marketable output sector increases, and the consumption of marketable output does not decline as a proportion of income, then the share of investment plus the trade balance must deteriorate.

National income measured by output is equal to the value-added of non-marketable output goods, marketable consumption goods, marketable investment goods, and the trade balance. If the output of non-marketable goods rises and the output of marketable consumption goods does not fall, then either investment or the balance of payments must suffer.

National income measured by types of income is equal to wages and profits (including dividends, interest, etc.) paid in the production of marketable goods, plus wages and profits paid in the production of non-marketable goods, plus the balance of payments surplus. If the wage bill in the non-marketable output sector rises, through the growth of employment or wage rate increases, then profits in industry and/or the balance of payments will suffer unless the wages bill in the marketable output sector falls. If profits fall, investment in industry will fall.

Bacon and Eltis claim that employment outside the marketable output sector rose by roughly one-third relative to employment in the marketable output sector from 1961 to 1974, apparently far in excess of other countries. Employment in education increased by 76 per cent, local government employment increased by 54 per cent, and central government employment by 10 per cent (all producing non-marketable output). Wages in these occupations also rose in excess of the average, and the effect on the economy as a whole was a fall in profits net of tax to the detriment of investment in the marketable output sector. Had the industrial base been strengthened by more investment in the marketable output sector, deindustrialization would have been considerably reduced and the overall macroeconomic performance of the economy would have been much healthier.

Weaknesses in the argument

There are several weaknesses in the argument. The essential task is to show that non-market activities have starved the manufacturing sector of resources – especially labour and investment funds – which would otherwise have been productively used in manufacturing.

On the labour shortage hypothesis, the Bacon and Eltis argument is not supported by the facts. Between 1966 and 1976, the labour shed by the manufacturing sector was mainly male whereas the labour employed in the public sector was mainly female. The manufacturing sector was not starved of labour by the growth of employment in the public sector.

As far as investment is concerned, it is possible that the resources required by a growing public sector could have reduced the funds available for profitable investment in the market sector. With labour productivity growing faster than the demand for output, labour will be shed from manufacturing unless there is investment in new and technologically advanced activities. Was there **crowding out** of investment from the private sector?

Table 8 Investment in the UK 1961–86

	Private-sector investment as a percentage of total	*Manufacturing investment at 1980 prices (£ million)*
1961	62	6592
1967	53	6322
1970	58	7990
1972	62	6345
1974	58	7432
1979	71	7496
1982	74	4685
1986	80	6329

Source: *Economic Trends*, Annual Supplement.

To examine this argument in more detail, Table 8 shows movements in the proportion of total investment accounted for by the private sector and the level of real manufacturing investment. The years shown represent peaks and troughs in the ratio of private to total investment. In 1961 private investment represented 62 per cent of the total, and by 1967 it had fallen to 53 per cent – the lowest point in the period covered. Up to 1972 it rose gradually to 62 per cent, falling slightly between 1972 and 1974 and then rising to 80 per cent in 1986. If Bacon and Eltis were correct then we would expect a gradual but constant downward trend in the proportion of investment stemming from the private sector. Apart from the period 1961–67 this does not appear to be the case. Perhaps more important is the fall in real manufacturing investment after 1970 – which picked up after 1972 before falling dramatically after 1979. This cannot be attributed to government claims on investment funds which in relative terms were mainly declining through the 1970s.

In the light of the evidence, it is hard to sustain the view that the growth of the non-market sector has been the cause of deindustrialization.

North Sea oil

Another explanation of the more recent demise of manufacturing industry concerns the discovery and export of North Sea oil. The argument is as follows.

Theory

Consider a small open economy such as the UK with two sectors: one sector producing goods which are traded internationally (which we assume to be the manufacturing sector) and a sector producing non-traded goods (assumed to be the service sector). Further assume that all factors of production are fully employed and mobile between sectors. The price P_t of tradeable goods relative to the price P_n of non-tradeables measured in a common currency is

$$P_t/P_n = eP_w/P_n,$$

where P_w is the world price of tradeables (measured, say, in US dollars) and e is the exchange rate measured as the domestic (sterling) price of dollars. Since the world price of traded goods is assumed fixed, the relative price of traded goods can only change if the exchange rate changes, or if the price of non-traded goods changes.

Now consider Figure 7 which shows the supply of exports and demand for imports in relation to the relative price of tradeables. At P_0 the balance of payments is in equilibrium. This equilibrium is then disturbed by the discovery and export of oil. The supply of exports curve shifts to the right (X_0 to X_1) since more exports will be forthcoming at a given relative price of traded goods. If the demand for imports remains constant (the full-employment assumption), then the relative price of traded goods falls to P_2 in order to establish a new equilibrium. This happens through the process of exchange rate appreciation. It can be seen, therefore, that in a static framework with the full employment of resources and flexible prices, the introduction of oil exports reduces the output of manufactured goods if the balance of payments is to remain in equilibrium. At P_2, exports of manufactured goods fall to OQ_2, with $Q_2 - Q_1$ representing oil exports.

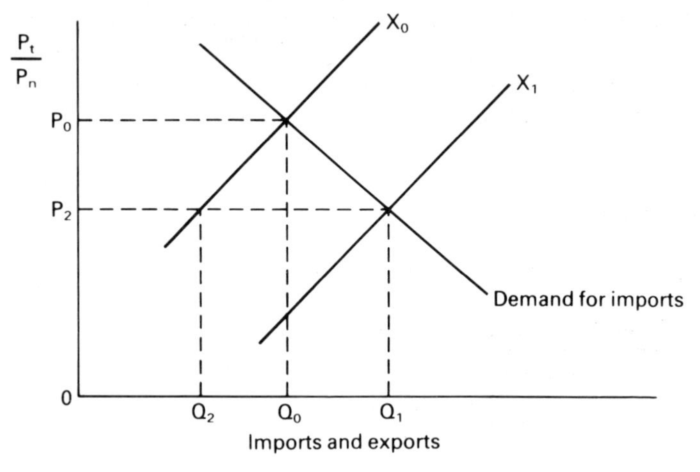

Figure 7 The supply of exports and demand for imports in relation to the relative price of tradeables

The facts

On the surface, this theoretical account of deindustrialization would seem to fit the facts of the late 1970s when oil production increased rapidly along with exports of fuels. As Table 9 shows, the extraction of North Sea oil (and gas) began in earnest in 1976 and grew rapidly thereafter, and by 1983 the volume of fuel exports was four times higher than in 1975. The effective exchange rate (i.e. the exchange rate relative to a basket of currencies), however, did not begin to appreciate until 1978, when fuel exports rose by 43 per cent in one year, suggesting that the impact of oil on the manufacturing sector could not have occurred until the very late 1970s.

There are, however, shortcomings in the theoretical model. There is nothing inevitable about a fall in the relative price of traded goods following a natural-resource discovery which earns foreign exchange. There are a number of ways in which additional foreign exchange can be used which would keep the relative price of tradeables at P_0 by preventing the exchange rate appreciating:

- it could be accumulated;
- it could be invested abroad;
- it could be used to buy more imports as part of a process of expansion, especially if the economy is *not* at full employment; or
- it could be invested as part of a growth strategy.

How the exchange rate moves is at the discretion of the monetary authorities. The fact that the exchange rate was allowed to rise in 1979 undoubtedly contributed to the contraction of manufacturing industry; but it was not the *inevitable* result of North Sea oil. In any case, the process of deindustrialization began in the 1960s, and as a long-term trend it has nothing to do with recent exploitation of North Sea oil.

If we consider long-run trends, a more convincing explanation lies in the weak trade performance of the UK manufacturing sector, particularly the slow growth of exports relative to the propensity to import, as outlined in the model earlier.

Table 9 The impact of North Sea oil (1980 = 100)

	Output of gas and oil	*Fuel exports*	*Fuel imports*	*Effective sterling exchange rate*
1975	0.3	33	150	104.1
1976	16.2	40	151	89.1
1977	47.4	55	125	84.6
1978	68.9	70	121	84.9
1979	98.7	100	119	90.0
1980	*100.0*	*100*	*100*	*100.0*
1981	110.3	121	82	98.9
1982	125.6	123	75	94.2
1983	137.6	148	67	86.7
1984	147.1	160	87	81.9
1985	150.3	171	86	81.8
1986	153.1	175	94	75.9
1987	149.2	173	95	75.7

Sources: *Monthly Digest of Statistics* (various)

The weak trade performance

The importance of manufacturing industry for the UK balance of payments has already been emphasized above. The balance of trade in manufactured goods has traditionally been in surplus, but the surplus has been gradually eroded since the mid 1960s (see Figure 8). In 1965, the value of exports of manufactured goods was more than 180 per cent of the value of imports, and by 1974 it had fallen to less than 120 per cent. Since then the trend has continued downwards with fluctuations towards the point where, in 1983, there was for the first time in history a deficit on the **balance of trade** in manufactured goods (see Figure 9).

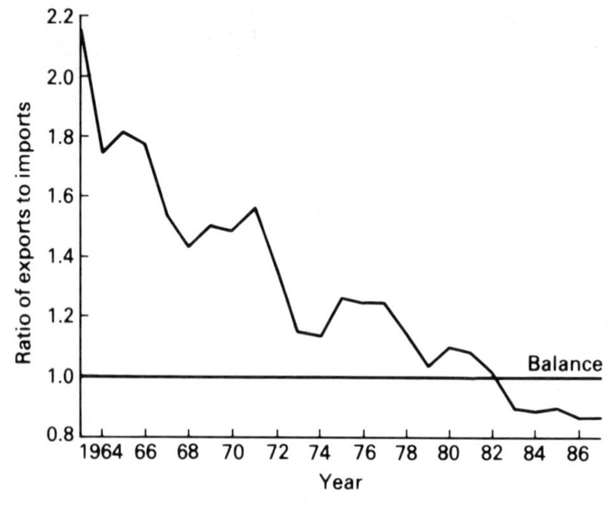

Figure 8 Balance of trade in manufacturing 1963–87

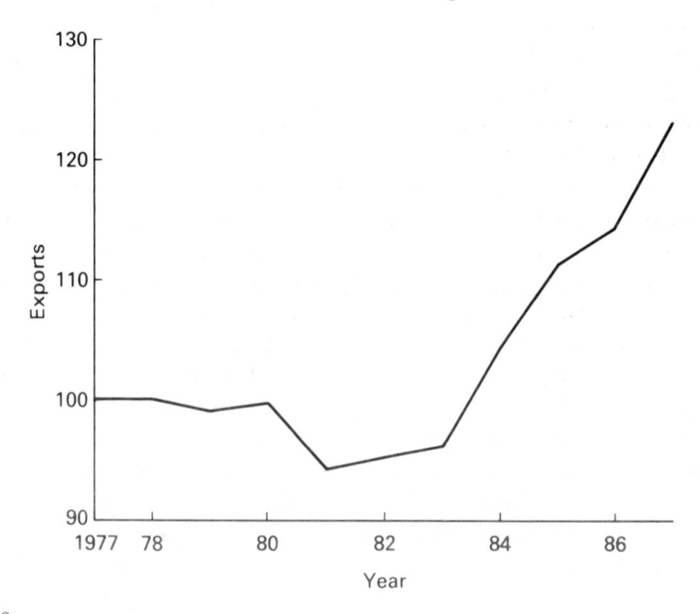

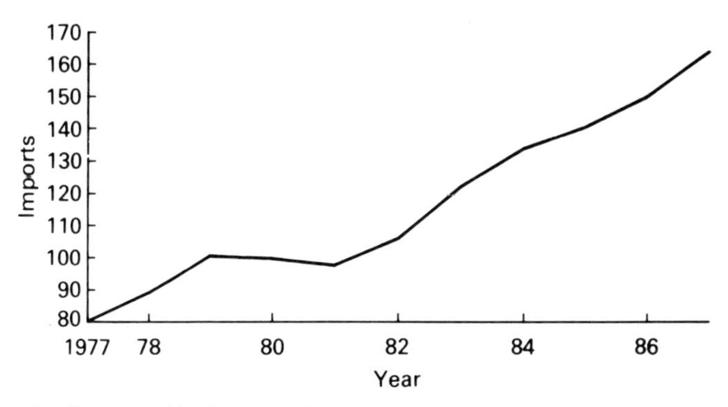

Figure 9 Exports (*facing page*) and imports of manufactures 1977–87

It is the weak trade performance of the manufacturing sector, reflected in the gradual elimination of the trade surplus, that provides the most convincing explanation of deindustrialization – measured in terms of the absolute, long-term decline in employment in the manufacturing sector. The fact is that UK manufacturers have not been able to sell enough, either at home or abroad, for the growth of output in manufacturing to exceed the growth of labour productivity, and inevitably employment has decreased. Exports have not grown fast enough, and imported manufactured goods have steadily penetrated the UK market.

Import penetration

To analyse the problem in more detail, Table 10 shows how **import penetration** – which reduces the growth of UK manufacturers' sales in the UK – has risen since 1968. In aggregate, foreign producers increased their share of the UK market for manufactured goods from 17 per cent in 1968 to 28 per cent in 1982, and further still by 1987. Sectors experiencing large percentage increases in import penetration were instrument engineering, electrical engineering and vehicles, where in each sector in 1982 the share of imports in the domestic market exceeded 45 per cent.

Table 11 shows exports as a proportion of manufacturers' sales for the period 1968–82. Between 1968 and 1979, each of the industries listed increased the share of its sales comprised of exports by, on average, eight percentage points. Seven of the seventeen industries increased the share of exports by more than ten percentage points, especially the three engineering sectors. Between 1979 and 1981, most industries further increased the share of exports in sales in spite of a small reduction in 1979.

Table 10 Import penetration in the UK: imports as a percentage of home demand

	1968	*1974*	*1979*	*1982*
Food, drink and tobacco	21	21	17	15
Coal and petroleum products	22	16	15	17
Chemicals and allied industries	18	27	30	33
Metal manufacturing	18	24	25	31
Mechanical engineering	20	28	32	35
Instrument engineering	30	50	56	62
Electrical engineering	14	29	38	49
Shipbuilding and marine engineering	–	57	36	17
Vehicles	14	23	40	45
Metal goods (NES)	5	10	13	15
Textiles	16	24	33	40
Leather, leather goods and fur	21	27	40	45
Clothing and footwear	12	20	30	35
Bricks, pottery, glass and cement	5	9	10	11
Timber and furniture	27	32	29	27
Paper, printing and publishing	17	23	20	22
Other manufacturing industries	10	16	19	24
Totals	17	23.3	25.8	28.4

Source: *Monthly Digest of Statistics* (various).

Table 11 Exports as a percentage of manufacturers' sales

	1968	*1974*	*1979*	*1982*
Food, drink and tobacco	4	5	6	6
Coal and petroleum products	13	14	14	17
Chemicals and allied industries	24	34	37	41
Metal manufacturing	15	17	21	27
Mechanical engineering	32	40	42	47
Instrument engineering	33	52	57	63
Electrical engineering	20	29	38	45
Shipbuilding and marine engineering	–	25	38	18
Vehicles	34	39	42	46
Metal goods (NES)	12	14	16	17
Textiles	18	25	30	32
Leather, leather goods and fur	25	28	29	35
Clothing and footwear	9	11	19	19
Bricks, pottery, glass and cement	9	13	14	13
Timber and furniture	2	5	7	7
Paper, printing and publishing	7	9	11	11
Other manufacturing industries	15	18	19	22
Totals	17	21.3	24.3	26.7

Source: *Monthly Digest of Statistics* (various).

This increase is deceptive, however, since increased import penetration has reduced the growth of home sales (and therefore the growth of total sales) of UK manufacturers, thus introducing bias into export performance when it is measured by the *share* of exports in total sales. Overall, there can be no doubt that the trade performance of the UK manufacturing sector has worsened considerably since 1968, and this is reflected in the gradual elimination of the trade surplus since the mid-1960s, while unemployment has grown.

Increasing deficit with the EEC

A further dimension of the problem is revealed in Table 12, which shows the balance of trade in manufactured goods with various blocs of countries. The most noticeable feature in the pattern of trade is the increasing deficit with countries in the European Economic Community since 1973, the year in which the UK joined the EEC. In 1970, the UK had a balance of trade surplus in manufactured goods with each bloc listed in Table 12 except with North America. By 1978, the UK had a trade deficit with each bloc except for 'other countries', and since then the position has worsened to the extent that after 1984 the trade surplus with 'other countries' was not sufficient to pay for the deficit with the EEC alone.

Table 12 UK balance of trade in manufactures with other blocs of countries 1970–87 (£ million)

	European Community	*Other Western Europe*	*North America*	*Other countries*
1970	+164	+457	−210	+1861
1972	−80	+285	+222	+1716
1974	−646	−50	−222	+2675
1976	−463	+295	−176	+4734
1978	−1615	−784	−147	+6464
1980	−1764	−182	−1465	+6979
1982	−4983	−1028	−1362	+7574
1984	−8350	−2439	−1153	+5544
1987	−11085	−2796	−1398	+5333

Source: *Overseas Trade Statistics* (various years).

What accounts for the overall weak trade performance of the UK manufacturing sector?

An obvious approach is to look at why the demand for UK manufactured goods at home and abroad has been relatively weak. In the foregoing analysis it was noted that demand depends on relative prices and income. A low demand for UK-produced goods may result, therefore, from a high relative price via the price elasticity of demand and/or a low income elasticity of demand in the presence of rising real income. The cause of the problem can therefore be analysed in terms, on the one hand, of **price competitiveness** and, on the other hand, the factors which make UK goods less desirable to consumers when their income rises.

Relative unit labour costs

Much emphasis has been placed on price uncompetitiveness as the reason for the poor trade performance of the UK manufacturing sector. This assertion is usually supported by a list of factors that have contributed to increased costs – such as trade union militancy, low productivity, inefficient management, low investment, high exchange rates and uncoordinated industrial policy. Each of these factors will contribute to increased costs, but first it is necessary to show that over a long period there has been a progressive reduction in competitiveness.

We need to look at the costs or prices of UK manufactured goods relative to those of other countries (with adjustment for exchange rate changes). A common measure of competitiveness is the **IMF index of relative unit labour costs**, which is shown for the period 1963–87 (along with **relative producer prices**) in Figure 10. Producer prices incorporate costs other than labour costs and may be a more representative index of competitiveness. An increase in either index represents a reduction in competitiveness as the cost of UK goods rises relative to the cost of foreign goods.

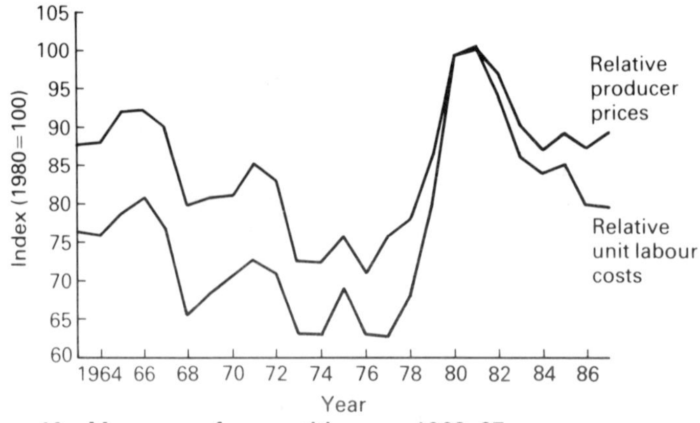

Figure 10 Measures of competitiveness 1963–87

In fact, between 1963 and 1976, the indices move in parallel on a *downward* trend. The competitiveness of UK products was improving, although not continuously. Following the effects of the 1967 devaluation, between 1968 and 1971 the indices rose but not back to their original levels. However, by 1976 both indices indicate that competitiveness had improved by over 20 per cent since 1966. After 1976, however, competitiveness fell dramatically. Each index rose significantly to reach its highest level (in the period shown) in 1981.

An argument difficult to sustain

As an explanation of the downward trend in the trade surplus in manufactured goods, the cost competitiveness argument is difficult to sustain. In the period 1966–76, cost competitiveness improved while the balance of trade surplus in manufactured goods diminished – the opposite of what might have been expected. It is only in the period after 1976 that the expected effect occurs, and we take a closer look at the events of the late 1970s and early 1980s in the next chapter.

Income elasticity of demand

But, in any case, cost competitiveness is not the only determinant of the demand. What is happening to income, and the characteristics of goods, are also very important. If income increases, demand will increase if the product in question is a 'normal' good. According to the concept of the **income elasticity of demand**, we can distinguish between 'necessities', where the income elasticity of demand is less than one (so that a 10 per cent increase in income is associated with an increase in demand of *less* than 10 per cent), and 'luxuries', where the income elasticity of demand is greater than one. A declining trade surplus in manufactured goods with improved competitiveness could occur if the goods produced by UK manufacturers in general possess a low income elasticity of demand, while those produced by competitors are 'luxuries'.

Given that the balance of trade in manufactured goods has not moved in the expected direction when competitiveness improved means that increases in income in the UK and abroad, combined with the income elasticity of demand, must have had an important impact. *It is to the factors that make the income elasticity of demand for UK exports of manufactured goods low, and the income elasticity of imports high, that we must look for the explanation of Britain's deteriorating trade performance in manufacturing.*

Non-price factors

Research undertaken by the National Economic Development Office (NEDO) points to the importance of **non-price factors** which have rendered UK manufactured goods in general less 'competitive'. Non-price competitiveness, which affects the income elasticity of demand, concerns such factors as: product quality and reliability, the standard of after-sales service, and delivery. The important determinants of non-price competitiveness are therefore expenditure on research and development (R and D) and the way in which products are marketed.

Yet to gauge the actual degree of non-price competitiveness is difficult. How is the quality of a product measured, for instance?

D. Connell (consult the reading list) argues that a purchaser chooses between goods on the basis of value for money and not simply on the basis of relative prices. If products are homogeneous there will, in the long term, be no differences in price and so prices must diverge for reasons of product heterogeneity. If this is so, then it would be expected that products of better quality or technologically superior would have a higher value per tonne.

Connell found that in 1975 West German manufacturers were earning around 60 per cent more per tonne from exports of mechanical engineering products than were British manufacturers, and he attributes this to non-price rather than to price factors. In addition to this, he found that UK manufacturing firms 'have treated exporting as a marginal activity, rather than integrating it fully into their operations', and operate mainly in the smaller, slow-growing international markets.

Summary conclusion

It is clear, then, that it is not primarily reduced cost competitiveness that has contributed to the diminution of the UK trade surplus in manufactured goods. In the longer term, non-price factors such as design, quality, marketing and other parts of the product package have contributed to a low income elasticity of demand for UK manufactured goods. The weak trade performance of the UK manufacturing sector has been due more to non-price factors than simply to price uncompetitiveness.

KEY WORDS

Production function	Import penetration
Process innovation	Price competitiveness
Product innovation	IMF index of relative unit labour costs
Marketable output	Relative producer prices
Non-marketable output	Income elasticity of demand
Crowding out	Non-price factors
North Sea oil	
Balance of trade	

Reading list

Bacon, R. and Eltis, W., *Britain's Economic Problem: Too Few Producers*, 2nd edn, Macmillan, 1976.
Clark, A. and Layard, R., *UK Unemployment*, Heinemann Educational, 1989.
Connell, D., *The UK's Performance in Export Markets*, NEDO Discussion Paper 6, 1979.
Thatcher, A.R., 'Labour supply and employment trends', in *Deindustrialization* (Blackaby, F., ed), Heinemann, 1979.
Thirlwall, A.P., 'The UK's economic problem: a balance of payments constraint', *National Westminster Bank Review*, Feb. 1978.

Essay topics

1. Why is technical progress not necessarily the enemy of employment?
2. Using one method of national accounting, show that an increase in non-marketable output implies a lower level of investment and/or balance of trade, unless marketed consumption falls.
3. What are the objections to the thesis of Bacon and Eltis that deindustrialization has been the result of an increase in the provision by government of non-marketed output?
4. What is the mechanism by which the production and export of North Sea oil is supposed to have led to deindustrialization in Britain post-1979?
5. How would you define the concept of 'uncompetitiveness' which is used as an explanation for the weak trade performance of manufacturing industry?
6. Why are income elasticities of demand for imports and exports so important for determining the trade performance of countries?

7. In 1988 the then Chancellor of the Exchequer, Nigel Lawson, said: 'Some may be puzzled why the existence of current account deficit is so newsworthy in the United Kingdom. The truth is that we are prisoners of the past.' Do you share his puzzlement? Explain your answer.

Data Response Question 4

The impact of automation on employment

Read the accompanying article from the *Guardian* of 7 February 1985 and answer the following questions.

1. Why does Nobel Prize winner Wassily Leontief argue that as technology develops there will be a shortage of workers?
2. Why will clerical workers fare badly in the future?
3. Which major skill is forecast to be in demand?
4. What is structural unemployment?
5. Why might structural unemployment develop?

If we adapt fast enough the jobs will still be there

WHAT SORT of future will our children really inherit? The most popular economic scenarios tend either to project an imminent paradise in which an abundance of human ingenuity provides for every unimagined want, or alternatively that society will be characterised by a growing gulf between ever richer haves and ever more deprived have-nots.

Neither millenarian vision is in the remotest sense likely, as a new and fascinating study by the Nobel Prize winning economist Wassily Leontief and his associates demonstrates conclusively.

Leontief shows, in a report from his Institute of Economic Analysis at New York University which is due to be published by the Oxford University Press later this year, that much of the conventional wisdom about the new technology is simply wrong.

Far from it being likely that machines will displace workers, it is more likely that there will not be enough workers to operate all the machines we will want.

Equally, the changing structure of the labour force will not be dominated by a decline in production workers, who will probably increase their share of jobs. But there will be a dramatic fall in office workers and a rise in the number of professionals.

"The Impacts of Automation on Employment 1963–2000" relies on Input–Output Analysis, a method clearly different from the more usual attempts to build computer models of the economy. It constructs a detailed picture of each sector of the economy, rather than just looking at the big aggregates like Gross Domestic Product which are all that is necessary for short-term forecasting.

This approach makes sense because most of the impact of new technology comes through its gradual adoption as one old process is phased out, and the new one phased in. The structure of the economy is like the proverbial oil tanker which takes 10 miles to change course.

But in order to make their conclusions still more robust, the New York researchers project two different scenarios. I am going to concentrate on the scenario which assumes a relatively rapid pace of technical change, partly because Leontief and Dr Faye Duchin believe it is the more realistic. The broad comparison between the occupational structure of the labour force in 1978 and in 2000 is shown in the cake charts.

The research of course looks at the United States economy, which starts with a slightly different occupational structure from our own. (For example, they have more farmers than we have.) However, the broad changes in the occupational structure between 1978 and 2000 will have their parallels in Britain and other developed economies even if the starting points look slightly different.

Several important social implications stand out. Production workers – the blue collar working class – do lose many of their existing jobs, but they are rehired in growing industries required to produce new equipment for the technological revolution.

The people who are really hammered are clerical workers whose share in the labour force declines from 17.8 per cent to 11.4 per cent as office automation gathers pace. There is simply enormous scope for improving office techniques.

At present, the average American office worker uses only $2,000 compared with $25,000 of capital equipment for a factory worker.

As Dr Duchin, a woman, points out, the implications of this change for economies like Britain and the

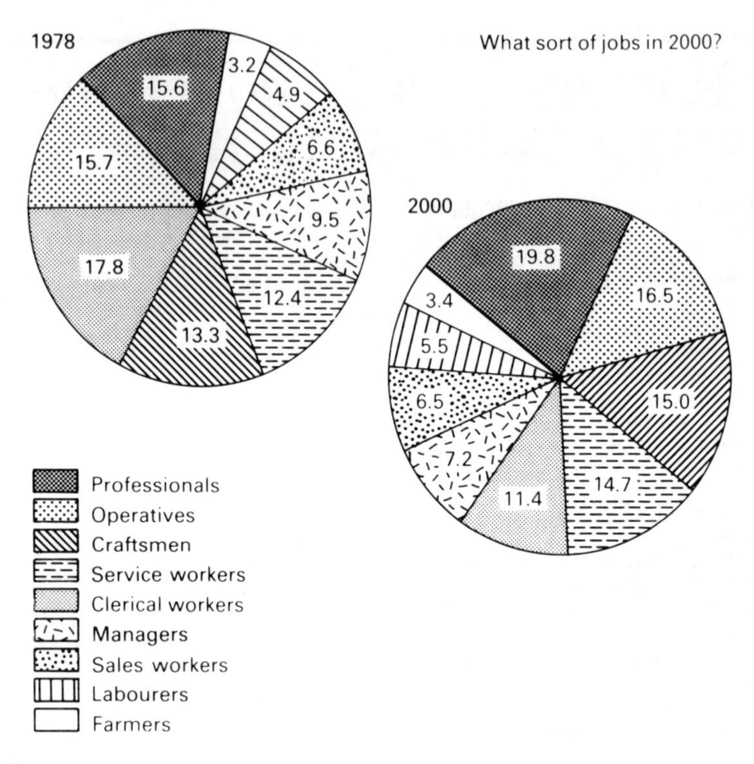

United States where there are a lot of women in the labour force – and a disproportionate number in clerical work – are that the trend towards more women working could be rapidly thrown into reverse unless women can adapt themselves to expanding occupations.

Maybe more will, Russian style, become labourers. Others will move into the gently expanding crafts or services. But the best bet for anyone is going to be the most rapidly expanding series of occupations of all – the professionals. And within the professional category, anybody with computer skills is going to be in great demand.

These calculations about the changing occupational structure are the ones about which the Leontief team feel most confident, but they also shed some light on the saloon bar wisdom that new technology is going to destroy jobs in aggregate (as opposed to destroying specific jobs).

When the researchers projected the growth of demand for various categories of goods and services as compiled by the US Bureau of Labor Statistics their favoured technological scenario simply generated too many jobs for what is likely to be the size of the American labour force in 2000. So they had to develop an alternative scenario which assumes a lower rate of technical change to create fewer jobs

In other words, the study strongly implies that the likely technological changes up to 2000 are going to increase the demand for labour rather than reduce it – exactly as past technological changes have done. If unemployment does stay high, it will be for other reasons such as the deflationary response of governments to wage bargainers' price-raising pay claims. It won't be due to new technology.

There are, though, some caveats to this conclusion at which I have already hinted. The forecast of final demand for goods and services is mainly assumed from the US government's projections rather than determined within the computer model itself. (The only element which arises from within the model is investment.)

However, these projections hardly seem unrealistic since national income grows by 2 per cent a year in the 80s and by 0.5 to 1.1 per cent a year in the 90s.

A more important caveat is that the job-creating effect of the new computer technology implies a lot of changing about within the overall total. But what if people do not, or cannot, train themselves up quickly enough to take the new job opportunities?

Other evidence shows that such structural unemployment is small now, but it is clearly still a possibility on the Leontief scenarios, which is why the researchers underline the importance of training, particularly at this stage, of the teachers. They point to a successful schools computer programme in France which spent 70 per cent of its budget allocation on teacher training and only 30 per cent on the actual "courseware" – in contrast with American experiences of going for the gadgets before the school teachers know how to use them.

One final caveat: the Leontief team has studied only the likely economic effects of computer based automation rather than, say, bio-technology. The latter, though, is likely to be of most impact in industries which are already capital intensive, with room for output expansion rather than labour saving.

What the Leontief study underlines heavily, though, is that all those who talk about technological change destroying jobs do so at their – and our – peril. The real moral is that the faster we adapt ourselves to the skills and the opportunities of technical change, the more likely we are to be able to enjoy lower unemployment and higher living standards.

Christopher Huhne
Economics Correspondent

Data Response Question 5

Testing theories of deindustrialization

Read the accompanying article from the *Times* of 2 December 1981 and the letter published in that newspaper on 11 December 1981. Answer the following questions.

1. Which of the five theories put forward to account for deindustrialization relate to the long-term trend and which to the recent experience?
2. Is 'stupid' a fair description of some of the economic policies pursued by government which have contributed to deindustrialization? Think of a defence.
3. Why does the Bacon and Eltis explanation of deindustrialization fail to explain the experience of the last decade?
4. What is wrong with the explanation that North Sea oil must cause an *absolute* contraction of manufacturing output and employment?
5. What do you understand by the 'New Cambridge' explanation of deindustrialization?
6. David Blake does not mention technical progress as a cause of deindustrialization. Do you think this is a mistake?
7. Can employment in service activities substitute for a decline in jobs in manufacturing?

Deindustrialization – testing theories

The huge drop in manufacturing output – down by more than a sixth since spring 1979 – has been the most striking feature of the recession. But in the debate about the Government's macroeconomic policies of the past two years, we often lose sight of the fact that the decline in manufacturing is not new.

It has been a persistent feature of the last eight years. In the mid-1970s it was identified by left and right as one of the country's prime economic problems. Many theories were put forward to explain why it was happening.

If we are to understand what is going on and what we ought to do about it, we ought to look again at some longer term explanations which have been put forward for what is going on in the industrial sector.

There are five main explanations of what has been happening which we should consider.

One is that the problems have been caused by stupid economic policies by the Government, which drove up the exchange rate through high interest rates, incited big pay rises by its tax policy and deflated the domestic economy by cutting its borrowing requirement.

Then there is the North Sea explanation, first put forward by Kay and Forsyth, which says that North Sea oil automatically causes a contraction in manufacturing output.

A third explanation is that of Bacon and Eltis, that growth of the public sector has led to contraction of manufacturing. The fourth is what is usually called the "New Cambridge" explanation, that growing imports eat up the British market and that conventional solutions, such as devaluation, will not stop this. Only import controls can meet the challenge under this scenario.

The fifth explanation is really the mirror image of the first. It says that contraction in manufacturing is a sign that the Government's policies have, at great cost, worked. Useless capacity which had been outdated by the 1973 oil shock has at last been removed and the industrial sector has become more efficient in response to competition.

As an explanation of what has happened in the past two years, the Bacon and Eltis explanation does not work. They argued that the sign of the deindustrialisation of Britain was the shift of workers from the trading to the public sector. By pre-empting resources the Government was effectively "crowding out" the private sector. Yet public employment has not risen in the past two years; it has fallen.

The million jobs lost in manufacturing have not been to the benefit of extra public service jobs; they have resulted in an increase in unemployment. Bacon and Eltis themselves warned that what was needed was not to cut the public sector but to boost the trading sector.

They wrote: "There would be the certainty of disaster if a Conservative pro-market sector government came to power and just sat back, balanced the budget and let unemployment mount waiting for the market to solve its problems."

What about the idea that North Sea oil has made a decline in manufacturing output inevitable. The argument rests on the fact that we export to pay for our imports. As we no longer have to pay for imports of oil, we can import more of other things and export less of our own manufactures. The manufacturing sector will therefore decline.

As a long term explanation this seems unsatisfactory. It is true that

the share of manufacturing in our national output would fall in those circumstances. But that is no reason why the absolute level should go down.

What we ought to expect, unless the domestic economy was at full capacity, would be that manufacturing would take a smaller share of a larger whole, but would not actually contract.

Oddly enough this inadequate explanation fits well in one respect with the experience of the past two years. One consequence of North Sea oil was to make sterling a more attractive currency. Supporters of the theory could argue that the pound went up in 1979 and 1980 because investors realized that Britain would get improving benefits to the balance of payments until 1985.

Yet the movements of the pound in 1981 hardly bear out the theory. When British interest rates were below world levels in the summer, the pound fell. Now that our interest rates are once again high, sterling is strengthening. This points strongly to the conclusion that the appreciation of the pound in 1980 owed more to British monetary policies than to a structural shift in the balance of payments.

What about the "New Cambridge" school of thought which ties deindustrialisation to rising imports? The problem here is that imports were falling at the same time that manufacturing went through the floor. As Sir Alec Cairncross pointed out, without accepting the Cambridge diagnosis of what should be done their definition of what deindustrialisation means has a lot to commend it. But over the past two years, it does not fit as a description of what has been happening.

Whether the Government was right to do what it did or not is something we can only tell in time; though if it was, it ought to be saying that the future lies with the growth of services, not telling workers to accept low pay settlements to hang on to jobs in manufacturing.

But it is a strange irony that a government whose election owed so much to a feeling that manufacturing had been treated too badly should have presided over the greatest industrial recession this century.

David Blake

Loss of jobs in manufacturing

From Professor A. P. Thirlwall

David Blake's article on deindustrialization was timely, but his analysis leaves a misleading impression in some respects. The absolute loss of jobs in manufacturing industry has been a persistent feature not only of the last eight years, but of the last 15.

Employment in manufacturing as a whole peaked in 1966 and has declined progressively by three million since then from nine million to six million, with a loss of one million in the last two years alone. This historical and recent decline is unparalleled in the world.

The argument that the growth of public-sector employment has been responsible for this worrying decline not only fails to explain what has happened in the last two years, but does not stand up to scrunity over the longer time scale. The "New Cambridge" argument, which ties deindustrialization to the inability of exports to pay for full employment imports, or in other words to a fundamental balance of payments constraint on output, cannot be discounted by saying that the "problem

here is that imports were falling at the same time that manufacturing went through the floor".

The depression of imports is itself a function of contraction which may still have had as one of its roots an imbalance between exports and plans to import.

As far as the longer term is concerned, my own work reveals a strong rank correlation across industries between the rate of employment decline and the rate of deterioration in the balance between imports and exports. A long-term solution to deindustrialization requires a foreign trade strategy based on the promotion of exports.

As far as the last two years are concerned, however, David Blake is correct that the loss of jobs can really only be satisfactorily explained in terms of the massive domestically engineered deflation of demand. It was pleasing to read in your same issue that at least one sinner at the London Business School has repented.

Yours sincerely,
A. P. THIRLWALL,
Keynes College,
The University,
Canterbury,
Kent

Chapter Six

The collapse of the manufacturing sector after 1979

'. . . *deindustrialization has produced serious structural imbalances in the British economy.*' M. Kirby

---

We pointed out in Chapter 2 that employment in manufacturing industry peaked in 1966, and since then it has been on a downward trend. In 1979, the Conservatives under Mrs Thatcher were elected to power after five years of Labour government, and Britain became a laboratory experiment for the application of the doctrine of **monetarism.** Very tight monetary and fiscal policy was pursued in order to 'squeeze inflation out of the system'.

Inflation did eventually abate, but the price was the deepest recession since the great depression of the early 1930s. The contraction of the manufacturing sector between 1979 and 1982 was unprecedented. Output fell by 16 per cent, investment fell by over 30 per cent, 1.3 million jobs were lost, and unemployment in the economy as a whole rose from 1.3 million to 2.8 million.

In this chapter, we first of all examine the factors that led to the collapse of the manufacturing sector in this period, and then go on to analyse why there has been no recovery of manufacturing employment even though there has been some recovery of manufacturing output and investment since 1983.

Explanations of the collapse

Figure 11 gives details of employment and output by sector over the period 1979–87. The indexed statistics show clearly that collapse of manufacturing output and employment was the main feature of the recession. There was some decline in output and employment in the service sector, but this was relatively small. If the loss of jobs in manufacturing between 1979 and 1983 had continued at the rate experienced between 1966 and 1979 (when about 150 000 jobs per annum were lost), employment in the manufacturing sector in 1983 would have stood at 6.5 million. The *actual* figure for that year was

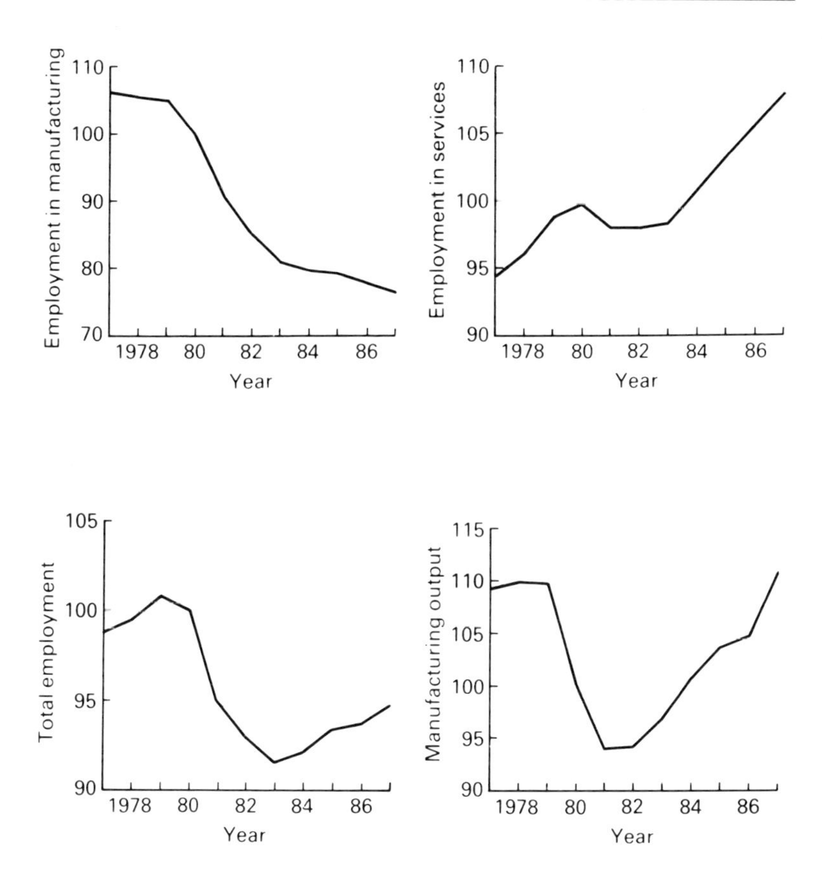

Figure 11 Trend lines for employment and output 1977–87 (indexed to 1980 = 100)

5.5 million. What happened in the early 1980s was not simply a continuation of past trends but an economic **shock.**

What are the explanations of this shock?

One popular view is that British manufacturing suffered unduly from the onset of **world recession** around about this time. The argument goes that for a long period manufacturing in the UK was inefficient, uncompetitive and over-manned. The world recession then forced a once-and-for-all shakeout of inefficient firms, and it is this which caused productivity in British industry to rise by 20 per cent between 1980 and 1983, and for relative unit labour costs to fall by 14 per cent over the same period. Such a *catharsis*, it was argued, was necessary, and that out of the ashes a phoenix would rise with British industry leaner and fitter, and better equipped to survive in an increasingly competitive international environment.

Does this explanation of events stand up to empirical scrutiny? There is no doubt that there was a severe world recession in the early 1980s. In 1980 world industrial production was stagnant, and during 1981 and 1982 it fell by 10 per cent. A close look at the timing of events in the UK, however, reveals that the collapse of the manufacturing sector was not *initiated* by the world recession. Recessions get transmitted from one country to another through the impact on trade, but the *volume* of world trade in manufactures continued to rise up to 1981 *after* manufacturing output in the UK had declined by some 14 per cent (see Figure 12). The world recession exacerbated the decline in output and employment after 1980, but the explanation of the collapse of manufacturing industry lies in factors affecting the UK manufacturing sector *before* 1980.

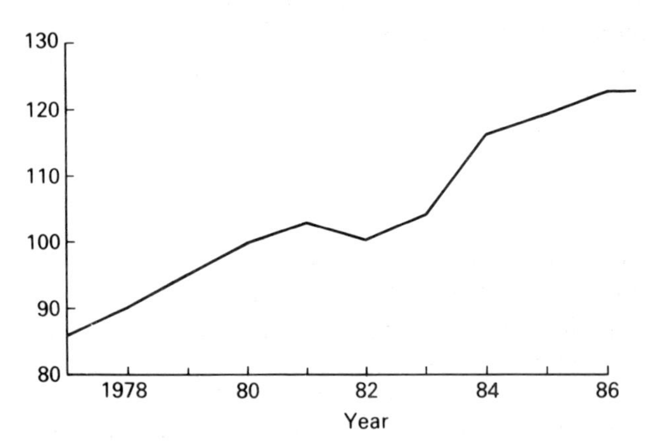

Figure 12 World trade in manufactures 1977–87 (Index 1980 = 100)

The first point to mention is that in the two years prior to 1979 there was a sharp deterioration in the balance of trade in manufactured goods to the tune of 17 per cent. The *volume* of imported manufactured goods rose by 25 per cent, while the *volume* of exports remained static (refer back to Figure 9). Manufacturing output increased by less than 0.5 per cent. As Professor Chrystal of the London Business School has pointed out (consult the reading list), UK manufacturers were being squeezed out of the domestic market; instead of reducing the scale of their operations immediately, they increased their stocks of goods (i.e. inventories), which rose by nearly 20 per cent up to 1980. It seems that they were expecting demand to revive, but this did not happen.

Why did demand remain depressed?

There were two major reasons why the demand for manufactured goods remained depressed from 1979 onwards. The first was the pursuit of a highly **deflationary economic policy** by the newly elected Conservative government in 1979.

The aim of the policy

The primary aim of economic policy became the control of inflation which showed signs of accelerating from an already high level with the collapse of incomes policy in 1978–79 under the previous Labour government. Inflation in 1978–79 was running at an annual rate of over 15 per cent, and wages were rising by over 20 per cent. The government's economic strategy involved cutting government expenditure to reduce the size of the government's deficit (or the so-called **Public Sector Borrowing Requirement** or PSBR) in the belief that this would help to curb the growth of the money supply from the supply side. According to monetarist doctrine, 'inflation is always and everywhere a monetary phenomenon' in a causal sense, and a sufficient condition, therefore, for the control of inflation is control of the money supply.

A so-called **Medium Term Financial Strategy** (MTFS) was introduced with the aim of controlling the growth of M3 money down to below 10 per cent. (MTFS also stands for Mrs Thatcher's Financial Squeeze!) At the same time, interest rates were raised to control the demand for money. The average short-term interest rate rose from 11.6 per cent in 1978 to 15.8 per cent in 1979, and the rate was kept high throughout 1981 and 1982. All this had a dramatic effect on the *internal* demand for manufactured goods, particularly through the adverse impact on investment demand which declined by over 30 per cent.

Exchange rate appreciation

The second important factor which depressed the demand for domestically produced manufactured goods was the rapid appreciation of the **exchange rate** in 1979 and 1980. Against the dollar, the value of sterling rose from $1.92 in 1978 to $2.33 in 1980 – a rise of over 20 per cent. Against a basket of currencies, the value of sterling (i.e. the effective exchange rate) rose by 18 per cent over the same short period

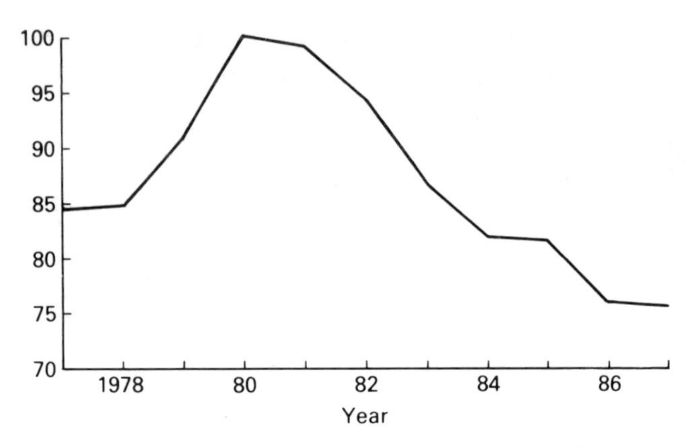

Figure 13 Effective Sterling index 1977–87 (1980 = 100)

(see Figure 13). Three major factors were responsible for this excessive appreciation:

- Firstly, in the late 1970s, increasing amounts of foreign exchange were being saved and earned by the production and export of North Sea oil. Between 1977 and 1979, fuel output doubled and exports increased by over 80 per cent (see Chapter 5 for full details).
- Secondly, high interest rates made sterling assets attractive for foreigners to hold, which added considerably to the demand for sterling.
- Thirdly, the recession (combined with North Sea oil) caused the *balance of payments on current account* to go into surplus – to the tune of over \$3 billion in 1980. This added to the demand for sterling relative to the supply; or to look at it another way, weakened the demand for foreign currency relative to the supply.

The effect of the exchange rate appreciation, however, was to switch demand from domestic to overseas suppliers of manufactured goods on a massive scale. There was an alarming increase in import penetration, and the balance of trade surplus in manufactured goods continued to diminish – until finally in 1983 it went into deficit for the first time in British economic history. The years 1979 to 1981 were an economic nightmare for manufacturing industry. Factories shut down, workers were laid off and the number of bankruptcies and insolvencies rocketed. As Professor Chrystal describes it:

> 'Domestic firms had lost their grip on the home market. There was no compensating expansion of exports. This increase in import penetration was

not due to an upsurge in incompetence on the part of domestic producers. Rather the explanation is found in the fact that this is the period of maximum expansion of North Sea oil.'

Unfavourable long-run trends

As we have argued, however, factors other than North Sea oil, and the impact of oil on the exchange rate, were also at work, including the continuation of unfavourable long-run trends. Indeed, according to econometric work undertaken for the House of Lords Select Committee on Overseas Trade (1985), 'longer term trends' were found to be as important as North Sea oil in accounting for the movement of the balance of trade in manufactures into deficit between 1977 and 1983.

The Select Committee was set up to examine the causes and implications of the deficit on trade in manufactured goods. Looking at the experience of the UK, hearing evidence from interested parties, including industrialists and academics, and examining the experience

Table 13 Components of the trade deficit in manufactured goods 1987* (£ million)

Standard International Trade Classification	*Exports (FOB)*	*Imports (CIF)*	*Balance of trade*
5–8: all manufactured goods	61 039	70 984	−9 945
5: Chemicals and related products	10 519.7	8 330.4	+2 189.3
6: Manufactured goods chiefly classified by material	11 877.3	16 970.3	−5 093.0
of which:			
64: Paper, paperboard and articles of paper pulp, of paper or of paperboard	971.1	3 238.2	−2 267.1
65: Textile yarn, fabrics, made-up articles (NES)	1 886.2	3 497.6	−1 611.4
7: Machinery and transport equipment	28 803.1	32 795.2	−3.992.1
of which:			
75: Office machines and automatic data processing equipment	4 483.2	5 431.2	−948.0
77: Electrical machinery, apparatus and appliances (NES)	3 786.1	5 051.8	−1 265.7
78: Road vehicles	4 876.8	8 807.2	−3 930.4
8: Miscellaneous manufactured articles	9 839.8	12 888.1	−3 048.3

* On an overseas trade statistics basis.
Source: *Overseas Trade Statistics*, December 1987.

of other advanced industrial countries, the Committee concluded that the continued decline of the manufacturing sector would 'constitute a grave threat to the standard of living of the British people. Failure to recognize [the] dangers now could have a devastating effect on the future economic and political stability of the nation.' The components of the trade deficit in 1987 are presented in Table 13.

Legacy of the collapse

The manufacturing trade balance in deficit, and getting worse, means that Britain's overall growth rate consistent with balance of payments equilibrium on current account is deteriorating; that is, the balance of payments equilibrium growth rate is falling, other things being equal (see Chapter 4). To put it another way, balance of payments deficits will emerge sooner and quicker as growth exceeds a certain level.

This appears to have happened with a vengeance in 1987 and 1988. With a growth rate of GDP in these two years averaging nearly 5 per cent a year, the current account of the balance of payments swung from balance in 1986 to a deficit of £15 billion in 1988.

Current account deficit on the UK balance of payments does matter

From Professor A.P. Thirlwall.

Every time I open the Financial Times I read Mr Samuel Brittan saying that Britain's current account deficit on the balance of payments does not matter, apparently on the grounds that it is being financed voluntarily by capital inflows. The current account deficit *does* matter, for two main reasons.

First, interest rates are higher than they otherwise would be. This has implications for investment and the modernity of the capital stock. To say that interest rates should be fixed at whatever level is necessary to restrain demand to "ensure that the current deficit is held at whatever the capital markets are willing to finance" seems to me to be quite irresponsible. It shows complete indifference to the level of output and employment.

Second, it is certainly true, as Mr Brittan says, that there is no law which states that all countries have to grow at the same rate. There is a law however, which says that every country will have a growth rate consistent with balance of payments equilibrium, and if growth exceeds that rate payments deficits will emerge.

Since the war, the UK has had the lowest growth rate consistent with balance of payments equilibrium of any major industrial country – which is why the UK has slipped from being one of the richest European countries to one of the poorest.

This may not worry Samuel Brittan, but it worries a lot of other

people. General indifference to the structural determinants of the current account of the balance of payments, and in particular to its components, has been a major cause of the deindustrialisation of the UK, with the consequences this has had for the loss of jobs and unemployment. Not until there is concern with the determinants of the current account, and particularly the balance of trade in manufactures, is there any hope of raising the growth rate consistent with balance of payment equilibrium, and reducing unemployment.

Samuel Brittan and the present government may put their faith in market forces, but there is precious little evidence, judging from the balance of payment figures, that the pursuit of *laissez-faire* for the last nine years has made any difference to the long-run underlying growth rate of the British economy consistent with payments equilibrium.

Lumping the capital and current account of the balance of payments together, and saying there is no problem because the balance of payments must always balance, is to bury one's head in the sand as far as the functioning of the real economy is concerned.

A.P. THIRLWALL
Keynes College,
University of Kent,
Canterbury, Kent

Figure 14 Letter to the Editor of the *Times*, 5 July 1988

The government and certain commentators do not regard the size of the deficit as a cause for concern (the letter reproduced as Figure 14 argues otherwise). Foreigners, it is said, are prepared to finance the current account deficit by holding UK financial assets, which create an offsetting surplus on the capital account (net of changes in reserves). Whether this situation can be sustained depends on overseas confidence in the management and performance of the UK economy. In particular, rising inflation or a currency depreciation will lead to capital losses for foreigners holding UK financial assets unless the rate of interest in the UK is raised to compensate for these losses. Increases in domestic rates of interest may restrain investment, which reduces aggregate demand and will undermine the future prospects of the UK economy. Interest-elastic consumer expenditures may also be reduced, which will reduce aggregate demand further.

If high interest rates are not sufficient to stave off a **sterling crisis** (in which foreigners withdraw their capital from UK assets causing the demand for sterling to fall), then drastic reductions in aggregate demand will be required to reduce imports and bring the current account back into equilibrium. This will in turn lead to higher unemployment. Without a reduction in the exchange rate, the growth rate consistent with balance of payments equilibrium on current account is now only approximately 1.5 per cent a year, which is not enough to reduce unemployment to levels experienced in the 1970s.

Coping with unemployment

Unemployment was on a rising trend in the UK throughout the 1970s. In 1970 unemployment stood at 0.25 million and had risen to 1.3 million by 1970. By 1982 it had doubled and eventually reached 3.3 million in 1986. It has since fallen, although part of the recorded reduction is due to fewer people claiming unemployment and related benefits rather than fewer people actually looking for work. (This is a consequence of changes made to how unemployment figures are collected.) In spite of arguments about the exact number of unemployed people, and how fast the number has been falling, it is clear that the collapse of the manufacturing sector has created an unemployment problem that is still to be cured.

Since employment in the manufacturing sector has continued to fall since 1982, unemployment will only be reduced if other sectors can grow fast enough, unless the size of the labour force falls. In the UK between 1983 and 1987 employment has risen only in parts of the service sector (see Table 14). In particular, sizeable increases in employment have occurred in the financial sector (0.45 million), in public administration, etc. (0.25 million) and in 'other services' such as hairdressing (0.3 million). Furthermore, there has been a net fall in male employment of some 60 000, while female employment has increased substantially by more than three-quarters of a million. Corresponding to these changes in the industrial and sex composition of employment is the marked increase in part-time work (defined as 30 hours or less per week). Of the three-quarters of a million jobs created (in net terms) since 1983, more than half have been for part-time workers.

To reduce unemployment further requires not only the creation of jobs for those currently seeking work, but also jobs for those entering the labour force in years to come. These will not only include those who have never worked before, but also those who rejoin the labour force as they perceive improvements in employment prospects (this is the so-called **encouraged worker effect**). In addition, if the manufacturing sector and other production industries continue to shed workers, then even more jobs elsewhere will need to be created. An important question, therefore, is to what extent can a sufficient number of jobs be created in the service sector to bring employment down to, say, less than one million? Taken together with the earlier argument that economic growth will be constrained by the current account of the balance of payments, the question can be rephrased as: *Can the UK economy recover to and sustain pre-1979 unemployment levels without a recovery of the manufacturing sector in terms of its* *contribution to trade and its contribution to employment?* We address this issue in the final chapter.

Table 14 Changes in employment in the UK 1983–87 (thousands)

	1983	*1987*	*1983–87*
Total	21 067	21 816	749 (3.5%)
Males	11 940	11 883	−57 (−0.5%)
Females	9 127	9 932	805 (8.8%)
Agriculture, forestry and fishing	350	321	−29 (−8.3%)
Coal, oil and natural gas extraction and processing	311	196	−115 (−37.0%)
Electricity, gas, other energy and water supply	338	301	−27 (−10.9%)
Manufacturing	5 525	5 145	−380 (−6.9%)
Construction	1 044	1 009	−35 (−3.3%)
Wholesale and retail distribution	3 155	3 353	198 (6.2%)
Hotels and catering	963	1 111	148 (15.3%
Transport and communications	1 345	1 345	– (–)
Banking, finance and insurance	1 875	2 328	453 (24.2%)
Public adminstration, education and medical services	4 804	5 055	251 (5.2%)
Other services	1 358	1 652	294 (21.6%)

Source: *Monthly Digest of Statistics*, November 1988.

KEY WORDS

Monetarism	Medium Term Financial Strategy
Shock	Exchange rate
World recession	Sterling crisis
Deflationary economic policy	Encouraged worker effect
Public Sector Borrowing Requirement	

Reading list

Lord Aldington, 'Britain's manufacturing industry', *Royal Bank of Scotland Review*, Sept. 1986.

Anderton, R., 'Current Account of the Balance of Payments', *Economic Review*, vol. 6, Jan. 1989

Chrystal, K.A., *Controversies in Macroeconomics*, 2nd edn, Phillip Allen, 1983.
House of Lords, *Report of the Select Committee on Overseas Trade*, HMSO, 1985 (summarized in *Economic Review*, vol. 3, Jan. 1986).
Smith, D., *Mrs Thatcher's Economics*, Heinemann Educational, 1988.
Turner, P., 'Change in the pattern of UK trade', *Economic Review*, vol. 5, Jan. 1988.

Essay topics

1. What, in your view, was the major explanation for the collapse of the manufacturing sector between 1979 and 1982?
2. Why did the sterling exchange rate appreciate so markedly between 1978 and 1980?
3. Do you agree that current account deficits on the balance of payments do not matter if they are 'voluntarily' financed by private individuals?
4. Is there any hope of reducing unemployment without a recovery of the manufacturing sector?
5. Since 1983 the rate of growth of productivity in the manufacturing sector has been very impressive. Employment, however, has continued to fall. Does this represent what was termed 'positive deindustrialization' in Chapter 2?
6. 'The 1980s have witnessed significant changes in labour productivity in the United Kingdom compared with the previous decade. These changes are most marked in figures for output per head, especially in the manufacturing sector where labour productivity has grown by 4.4% per annum on average in the 1980s compared with 2.3% for the 1970s. . . . If a significant change in productivity performance has occurred, this is an important element in an improvement in the supply side of the economy with, in turn, implications for trade performance and inflation' (*Bank of England Quarterly Bulletin*, February 1989). If this claim is true, is it a cause for celebration, concern or both?

Data Response Question 6

A reasonable trade-off

Read the accompanying article from the *Financial Times* of 1 February 1989, which was written by a Research Fellow in Economics at King's College, Cambridge. Answer the following questions.

1. Define 'internal' and 'external' balances.
2. What is a 'sustainable recovery'?
3. What would such a recovery require?
4. Define 'current account'.
5. What is a 'shock' in economics?
6. Explain in one paragraph: (a) 'A sustainable recovery would imply movement in a north-westerly direction'; (b) 'The authorities will be forced to consider moving back to the north-east'.
7. To what extent is the figure a visual summary of the theme of this book?

Trying to arrive at a reasonable trade-off

Conventional wisdom holds that rapid deterioration of Britain's current account is merely a reflection of a temporary surge in the growth of domestic demand. It does not, therefore, raise serious doubts about the durability of the economic recovery.

I would argue that this is far too optimistic a view. There is no evidence that a sustainable recovery has taken place. On the contrary, unless something changes, the level of unemployment will have to rise again towards – and even past – 3m. The problem is the old one of reconciling internal and external balance. For most of the past 70 years Britain has had to trim domestic economic policy with an eye to maintaining a precarious international and trading position. The evidence suggests that we face the same policy dilemma today.

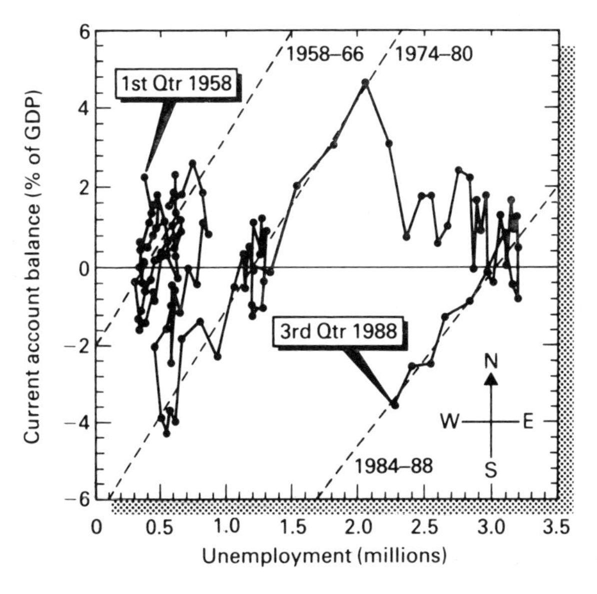

Consider the figure, which plots the current account balance (as a percentage of GDP) against unemployment for the past 30 years. Two things stand out. First, during short periods, there appears to be a trade-off between external balance – in the shape of a healthy current account – and internal balance, as measured by the level of unemployment. Second, over time, there has been a striking deterioration in the terms of this trade-off.

Thus, between 1958 and 1966 (when the relationship was admittedly a rather weak one) unemployment of about 380,000 was compatible with current account balance. During the late 1960s and early 1970s, the trade-off progressively worsened so that unemployment had to be about 750,000 for external balance.

The oil shock of 1973 exacerbated existing problems. By the beginning of 1974 the level of unemployment consistent with current account balance had jumped to 1,221,000. This new trade-off – represented by the middle line on the diagram – held good until the first quarter of 1981 despite the dramatic transformation of Britain from oil importer to oil exporter. It suggests that the rise in unemployment during 1980 and early 1981 was, to some extent, a policy choice and that the *underlying* (zero current balance) rate was still just over one million.

But during the following three years matters deteriorated very badly. Even though the current account stayed in surplus, the cost in terms of unemployment grew. This meant that when domestic demand revived and unemployment began to fall, the current account quickly went into deficit. Between 1981 and 1984 (see the right-hand line in the figure) the level of unemployment consistent with current account balance rose to just under 3m.

There is no evidence that the present recovery is upsetting this pattern. A sustainable recovery would imply movement in a north-westerly direction, off the regression line using 1984–88 data. So far the movement has been south-westerly. It could be argued that a deteriorating external balance is no longer a cause for concern since British residents now own substantial foreign assets and foreigners appear willing to invest in the UK. Evidence for this may be sought in the relative strength of sterling, even in the face of poor current account performance.

The asset position, which resulted from the policy choice to translate oil exports into current account surpluses rather than into an expansion of the domestic economy in the early 1980s, has given room for manoeuvre on the external account. There has certainly also been an important but unquantifiable "Thatcher" confidence effect at work.

The fact remains, however, that the current account will, eventually, assert itself. If the underlying competitive position of the economy does not soon improve – in other words if there is no movement in a north-westerly direction in the figure – the authorities will be forced to consider moving back towards the north east. The Government can certainly reduce the current account deficit by accepting more unemployment, but it is unclear what it can do to improve the terms of this trade-off.

Policy changes which exploit a short run trade-off between internal and external balance are well understood. But structural shifts in the trade-off itself are more puzzling. What has caused the long-run deterioration in the terms of the trade-off between unemployment and current account balance? In terms of the diagram, why have the regression lines shifted towards the right? There have been two or perhaps three structural shifts of importance: the first in the late 1960s and early 1970s; the second during 1973 and 1974; the third between 1980 and 1984.

Of these the second is easiest to understand since it was an obvious consequence of the oil shock. Comparing the other two, it is clear that what happened in the early 1980s –

an increase in the underlying unemployment rate of 1.8m – was several times more serious than the corresponding increase of 370,000 between 1966 and 1972.

But despite the difference in scale, the same mechanism was at work. In both periods the output and capacity of manufacturing industry declined. The collapse was dramatic in the early 1980s, but it is also possible to detect significant deterioration in the mid-1960s and again in the early 1970s.

A deterioration in the terms of the trade-off between current account balance and unemployment has thus occurred at times when investment in manufacturing has been insufficient to provide the production capacity needed in a fully employed economy. Attempts to run the economy too close to full employment without the necessary manufacturing capacity have inevitably led to a deteriorating trade balance in manufactures. While other components of the current account – such as oil – can mask this effect for a period, they cannot provide a long-term respite.

Those who insist on being optimistic can adopt one of two positions. They can dismiss the current account altogether as an indicator of performance or constraint on policy. Adherents of this view are quite happy to sail off in a south-westerly direction in the figure, and do not fear the consequences.

Optimists of the second type do acknowledge the existence of past and present trade-offs between domestic activity and external balance, but they believe the current recovery will lead to a more competitive economy. Just as the policy choices of the early 1980s led to the accelerated scrapping of equipment and a worsening trade-off between unemployment and current account balance, so the present boom will induce investment in new, efficient plant and shift the whole trade-off back to left in the figure.

In principle, there is something in this. The problem is the scale of new investment required to enable British manufacturing to compete internationally and meet enough of domestic demand to allow the economy to be run at near full employment.

There is little evidence that such investment is forthcoming and none that other sectors can fill the gap. Unfortunately, the likely outcome is that long before domestic investment reaches the necessary levels, the authorities will find it necessary to do more to discourage the boom, thus disappointing optimists of both schools.

Terry O'Shaughnessy

Chapter Seven

Policy implications

No attempt has ever been made in the UK economy to develop a coherent strategy of export-led growth.

If the process of deindustrialization is to be halted, the trade performance of the manufacturing sector needs to be improved. There are three possible routes:

- improving competitiveness;
- restricting the growth of imports; or
- increasing the rate of growth of exports.

Improving competitiveness

One of the main policy instruments in this context is the exchange rate. An exchange rate depreciation will improve the balance of trade in manufactures provided the demands for exports and imports are sufficiently price-elastic. The specific condition is that the sum of the price elasticities of demand for exports and imports sum to greater than one (the **Marshall–Lerner theorem**). The effect that exchange rate depreciation has on the balance of trade, however, is also dependent on other policies being pursued at the same time, particularly on monetary policy. For example, if a high interest rate policy is being pursued to restrict the demand for credit, this may worsen competitiveness by increasing costs and reducing investment (as well as attracting short-term capital inflows which will tend of offset the depreciation).

The relevance of exchange rate depreciation can also be questioned. Currency depreciation tends to ossify an industrial structure by making countries more competitive in types of goods that may be responsible for balance of payments difficulties in the first place (i.e. the production of 'down-market' goods). Moreover, depreciation would have to be continuous to put a country on a higher *growth* path consistent with balance of payments equilibrium, and it is also highly inflationary: by raising the price of traded goods. As many authors have shown, depreciation cannot be relied upon to improve competitiveness or to rectify balance of payments disequilibrium for a sustained, long time period.

Competitiveness will also be improved if unit labour costs fall relative to other countries. Labour costs per unit of output depend on the money wage rate and the level of labour productivity. If money wage rates can be restrained and labour productivity increases, competitiveness may improve. **Supply side policies** aimed at making the labour and product markets more competitive are regarded by some as being aimed at restraining wage inflation and improving efficiency (see Levačić, 1988).

Protectionism

Import controls are a possibility but there are many weaknesses and disadvantages of an inward-looking strategy based on import protection.

Firstly, if import controls take the form of tariffs, a once-for-all tariff may reduce the *level* of imports, but it is unlikely to reduce the *rate of growth* of imports permanently, which is what is required if the country is to move to a higher growth path without balance of payments difficulties arising. To reduce the rate of growth of imports permanently would require an ever-increasing tariff level in the same way that it is recognized that a *continual* depreciation of the currency would be necessary to achieve the same objective if that were a feasible policy.

Secondly, if price uncompetitiveness is part of the problem, tariffs are a policy of adjusting the **internal price structure** to the **internal cost structure**, while what is required is an adjustment of the internal cost structure to the **external price structure**. The danger is then that once the limits of import substitution have been reached there is no basis for further improvement in the balance of payments. Faster export growth is jeopardized and virtually precluded because an unfavourable internal cost structure has been protected. Many developing countries have paid dearly for this **import substitution strategy** at the expense of promoting exports. If demand is at all important for achieving high levels of output and productivity, and for reaping economies of scale, it is much more sensible to orientate domestic industry to the virtually unlimited world market, as Japan learnt to do a long time ago, and which countries like Korea, Singapore and Taiwan have also learnt to do.

A third disadvantage of tariffs is that, by raising the internal price level, a loss of consumer welfare is incurred. It is true that the revenue gained from tariffs could be used to reduce indirect taxes on goods but there is no guarantee that this would happen.

An alternative form of import control would be **import quotas**. To be effective, however, in reducing permanently the rate of growth of imports, they would have to be comprehensive covering virtually all imports. Otherwise, as demand was expanded there would be some switching from imports with quotas to imports without, and imports would continue to grow. There could also be complex administrative problems in allocating the scarce imports between competing uses.

Whatever form import controls take, however, they are all isolationist and inward-looking. A dynamic growth and development policy cannot be based on protection alone. There must be an **export strategy** as well. The counter-argument to these criticisms has three elements:

- Firstly, import controls work quickly to get an economy back to full employment.
- Secondly, in the movement back to full employment, investment will rise, technological progress will accelerate and average costs of production will fall, producing dynamic benefits which will raise the rate of growth of exports.
- Thirdly, if controls discriminate against countries with a balance of payments surplus this will help to raise the growth of world income and consequently UK exports too.

There is some force in this counter-argument, but it requires a very much greater act of faith to believe in dynamic benefits stemming from import controls than in the benefits that could accrue from an investment and taxation policy deliberately orientated to raising the rate of growth of exports. The dynamic benefits from import controls are supposed to arise as firms move along downward-sloping average-cost curves towards full capacity utilization. There can be little doubt that cost curves are downward-sloping at less than full employment, but what happens under this strategy when full employment is reached and there is no more scope for import substitution? The dynamism produced by import restrictions ceases. By contrast, an investment policy to encourage exports, which also relieved the balance of payments constraint on demand, would also move firms along the same downward-sloping cost curves; but at the same time, by inducing structural change, the policy could put exports and hence the economy on a permanently higher growth path. Import controls and import substitution may be a quicker route to full employment than an industrial strategy to raise exports, but they are inferior as a growth strategy if export growth remains unchanged.

The policy of import restrictions will also no doubt help to raise the growth of world income provided the composition of imports is altered against those countries with balance of payments surpluses. However, if the world income elasticity of demand for UK exports is lower than for other countries (which it is), a rise in the growth of world income will *worsen* the *relative* performance of the UK economy. In other words, a policy of import restrictions does nothing to raise the propensity of other countries to buy UK goods and thus would simply consolidate the UK's position at the bottom of the growth league table as far as exports are concerned. By contrast, if an investment strategy, working through the tax system, could induce structural change in favour of activities producing goods with a high income elasticity of demand in world markets, the growth of world income would be raised in the same way as under import controls (by relieving the economy of the balance of payments constraint on demand), and at the same time the growth rate of UK exports would be higher and hence the overall growth of output.

Those who advocate import controls are understandably preoccupied with the short-run, but there is also a need to stand back and to consider the longer-run issue of the UK economy's chronically slow underlying average growth rate over the post-war years compared with other developed countries. All the evidence suggests that a necessary condition for a faster long-run rate of growth of output and living standards is a faster rate of growth of exports, which import controls do nothing to foster directly. If intercountry differences in export and import propensities are examined, it is not so much the overall UK import propensity which looks so alarming but the abysmally slow growth of exports compared with other countries. This, in turn, seems to have very little to do with relative price differences, but with a very low income elasticity of demand for UK goods in world markets owing mainly to the supply characteristics of the goods such as their design, reliability, delivery, marketing, servicing and quality in the widest sense.

Regardless of 'quality', we also know that some goods have an intrinsically lower income elasticity of demand because they are 'inferior' goods (goods produced to cater for low-income markets as opposed to high-income markets). There is no hope of improving this fundamental weakness by import controls (or by currency depreciation for that matter).

An import control strategy would also, of course, run directly counter to the **Treaty of Rome** and jeopardize Britain's membership of the EEC. A more promising and acceptable approach to Britain's foreign trade weakness would be to promote exports.

Export-led growth

No attempt has ever been made in the UK economy to develop a coherent strategy of export-led growth. The primary task of economic policy in the United Kingdom must be to develop a strategy of export-led growth based on a judicious mix of taxes and subsidies to alter the allocation of investment resources and the composition of output in favour of exports. UK export performance is a function of the *types* of goods produced and the *division* of output between domestic and foreign markets. **Tax incentives** could be used both to alter the structure of production and to raise export performance within the structure. The **structural change** required is to induce an allocation of resources in favour of technologically progressive industries producing goods with a high income elasticity of demand in world markets. The policy could be integrated with an **industrial strategy** and linked to a system of **investment grants** and allowances. Investment incentives could be discriminatory according to various growth criteria.

A complementary strategy – or a second-best to the first if the idea of discrimination offends the British sense of fair-play – would be to relate investment grants and allowances to the proportion of output exported. This would tend to bias both the structure of output and the composition of output towards exports if manufacturers are at all responsive to differential rates of return. In addition, it would be possible simply to make exporting more profitable by remitting corporation tax on export earnings.

A number of other things could be done: exporting firms might be offered cheaper credit for investment; an attempt could be made to raise the status of marketing in firms; encouragement could be given to foreign-language training, and to finding room for engineers in the board-rooms of firms.

Such an export-led growth strategy, however, violates international trading agreements – in particular, Article 92 of the Treaty of Rome which lays down that state aids which distort competition are incompatible with the Common Market. It does specify, however, two forms of permissible 'regional' aid: (1) aid intended to promote economic development in regions where there is a low standard of living or serious under-employment, and (2) aid intended to facilitate the development of *particular activities* or economic regions, provided that it does not affect trading conditions adversely. In one sense, any subsidy or tax concession to any activity distorts 'free competition'. On the other hand, free competition itself may affect trading conditions adversely if it means that a country languishes economically and under-utilizes its resources. In these circumstances, support for activities to achieve a fuller utilization of resources could enhance the volume of trade for all. It is in this spirit that support for export activities within regional groupings should be assessed.

It is interesting to note that Article XII of the **GATT agreement**, originally signed in 1948, permits control over imports for the same balance of payments reasons, and countries adversely affected are not permitted to impose counter-measures. Given the UK's long-term economic dilemma and the massive full-employment deficit on the current account of the balance of payments, one might hope that there would be a good deal of international sympathy for the kind of strategy here outlined, whether Britain remains a member of GATT and the EEC or not. At least the water could be tested, as other EEC countries have done from time to time with respect to both import restrictions and export promotion. Just how far a weak country could go would be interesting to see.

As 1992 is approached and the creation of a single European market, some mechanism will be required to permit countries to deal with structural balance of payments problems and the associated poor economic performance.

KEY WORDS

Competitiveness	**Import quotas**
Marshall–Lerner theorem	**Export strategy**
Supply side policies	**Treaty of Rome**
Protectionism	**Export-led growth**
Import controls	**Tax incentives**
Internal price structure	**Structural change**
Internal cost structure	**Industrial strategy**
External price structure	**Investment grants**
Import substitution strategy	**GATT agreement**

Reading list

Levačić, R., *Supply Side Economics*, Heinemann Educational, 1988.

Robinson, B., 'How fast dare we grow?', *Economic Review*, vol. 5, March 1988.

Thirlwall, A.P., *Balance of Payments Theory and the UK Experience*, 3rd edn, Macmillan, 1986.

Essay topics

1. Why do some economists advocate import controls as a means of revitalizing the manufacturing sector?
2. What are the main disadvantages of import controls as a method of halting the process of deindustrialization?
3. How could the tax system be used in the UK to promote export-led growth?
4. Think of imaginative schemes for improving Britain's export performance.
5. If Britain cannot pursue an independent economic policy to aid its manufacturing industry, should Britain stay in the EEC?

Data Response Question 7

A Far Eastern model?

Read the accompanying article from the *Guardian* of 11 December 1985, and answer the following questions.

1. Explain why 'high interest rates and high exchange rates do not help competitiveness'.
2. Do you agree that neglect of non-price factors has significantly contributed to the weak trade performance of the UK manufacturing sector?
3. Briefly summarize the 'history' which, in the authors' view, suggests that 'leaving the problem to the market will achieve nothing'.
4. Why is sterling depreciation inflationary? (Use arithmetic examples as proof).
5. Can you think of particular industrial categories that would benefit from a strategy of export promotion along the lines of the Far Eastern countries mentioned?
6. What kind of export promotion would you advocate?

Let's save manufacturing jobs by copying Korea and Japan

THIS WEEK'S report from the all-party Treasury committee of the House of Commons expressed its concern that the government's use of a high exchange rate to bring inflation down would "lead to a significant deterioration in the competitiveness of British manufacturing, and a loss of foreign and domestic markets".

The report echoes the similar concern of the House of Lords committee on trade, and represents a warning which ministers – and any future government – ignore at their peril.

The long-term contraction of the UK manufacturing base has been caused by a gradual erosion of the balance of trade surplus in manufactured goods since the mid-1960s, which culminated in the first recorded deficit in 1983. If the economy is ever to grow at a rate sufficient to reduce unemployment a trade strategy which concentrates on the manufacturing sector is urgently needed.

This is, first, because any period of sustained, unemployment-reducing growth is likely to cause the balance of payments to deteriorate, and exports of services will not be able to fill the gap left by a declining surplus of oil. Second, given the current trend of job creation in the service sector, unemployment is unlikely to fall below three million before the end of the decade without a substantial increase in employment in manufacturing. A trade strategy aimed at improving the trade performance of the UK manufacturing sector will need to be at the heart of any programme of job creation.

Due largely to the declining trade surplus in manufactured goods since 1966, employment in manufacturing fell from a peak of 9.1 million in 1966 to 5.5 million in 1984. During the period 1966–77 much of this loss was offset by a growth of employment in the services sector of about 227,000 jobs per annum but since then this has not occurred.

Between 1978 and 1984, employment in manufacturing fell by 1.8 million which, together with smaller reductions in employment in the construction industry and elsewhere, and a rise in the size of the labour force of over 600,000, caused unemployment to increase dramatically.

Since 1982, an average of 137,000 jobs per annum has been created in the services sector (while employment in manufacturing has continued to fall). But this is well below the rate required, given the expected increase in the labour force of around 800,000 between now and the early 1990s, if unemployment is to fall. Jobs must also be created in the manufacturing sector.

Government policy now appears quite contrary. On the one hand, it urges greater competitiveness through lower wage rises. On the other, it claims credit for those rises and at the same time has presided over a sharp 9 per cent loss of price competitiveness in the second quarter, due entirely to the rebound of sterling.

High interest rates and high exchange rates don't help competitiveness, although it is clear that price competitiveness is not the only factor determining the domestic and foreign demand for British goods.

In the long run, price differences for identical or very similar products will be eliminated and the strength of demand will reflect non-price factors such as quality, design, reliability and after-sales service. These attributes are particularly important as consumption moves away from "inferior" products and towards those of high quality as real incomes rise.

The weak trade performance of the UK manufacturing sector in the long term has been due more to neglect of these non-price factors than to price uncompetitiveness. For example, between 1966 and 1977, competitiveness improved by more than 20 per cent while the trade surplus in manufactured goods fell by more than half. Improved price competitiveness may be necessary, but it is certainly not sufficient to improve the balance of trade in manufactured goods in the long run.

One of the most debated points of the House of Lords committee's report is the role of services, of which only 20 per cent are apparently tradeable. While it is true that the service sector exports represent a small proportion of its gross output, this is not the essential point. It is a fundamental truth that no economy in the long run can grow faster than the rate consistent with balance of payments equilibrium, which is determined by the growth of exports (in volume terms) relative to the propensity to import as real GDP rises.

Between 1975 and 1984, exports of services in volume terms grew by only five per cent compared with 21 per cent for manufactured goods. The fact is that there is more scope for a higher rate of growth of exports of manufactured goods. The growth that can be expected in exports of services will not even fill the gap left by the declining trade surplus in oil, let alone raise the rate of growth of GDP consistent with balance of payments equilibrium. A trade strategy is required and it needs to be directed at the manufacturing sector. History suggests that leaving the problem to the market will achieve nothing.

The long-term erosion of the trade surplus in manufactured goods has been caused by a combination of substantial import penetration of the home market, and a slow growth of exports abroad. A trade strategy needs to halt or slow the rise in import penetration and increase the rate of growth of exports. A policy of currency depreciation will not affect those non-price factors that need to be improved if UK manufactured goods are no longer to be treated as "inferior."

Furthermore depreciation is inflationary, and if it is to raise the *growth* of exports the currency will have to be depreciated continuously. Another policy option is import restrictions through tariffs or quotas. While import penetration may be curbed there is a limit to which domestically produced goods can be substituted for imports after which the restrictions can do little to alter the rate of growth consistent with balance of payments equilibrium.

The idea of export-led growth is not a new one. Since the immediate post-war period, however, the UK has not had a purposeful strategy to promote the growth of exports.

The manufacturing sector needs to shift the structure of production towards exports and this could be achieved through the tax system and the allocation of industrial assistance.

If the UK economy is to recover sufficiently to reduce unemployment to pre-1979 levels, the shrunken manufacturing base will need to be rejuvenated. A strategy of export promotion which has been of vast benefit to such countries as Japan, Korea, Singapore and Taiwan, will help to achieve this. Without a trade strategy any programme to reduce unemployment significantly by the early 1990s will not be sustainable.

Anthony Thirlwall
Stephen Bazen

Chapter Eight

The future

'The improvement of UK performance depends both on an improved allocation of resources for invention and innovation and a much more efficient exploitation of the potential advantages to be derived from technical innovation.' C. Freeman

In Chapter 6 the events and consequences of the recession of 1979–82 were examined. It appears that the economic policy of the present government is to rely on the economy to self-correct. This essentially non-interventionist approach relies on the private sector to bring the economy back to its pre-1979 state, with the government pursuing supply-side policies to reduce the fiscal and bureaucratic burdens on businesses, to liberalize product markets and to remove 'imperfections' in the labour market. Macroeconomic policy seems to revolve around keeping inflation under control and ensuring that the confidence of owners of sterling assets is not undermined in order to finance the current account deficit.

In the **real economy**, various improvements are noticeable. Firstly, output per head in manufacturing industry has increased substantially. Between 1980 and 1986 output per head rose by 35 per cent, compared with 17 per cent for the whole economy. While this is impressive, the level of productivity in the UK continues to lag behind that of other advanced industrial countries such as the USA, Germany, France, Sweden and Italy.

Secondly, investment and output in manufacturing are now back above their 1979 levels. These improvements have not led to an increase in manufacturing employment since output growth has been outstripped by productivity growth.

Thirdly, the rate of growth of real GDP has increased and unemployment has fallen from its high in 1986 to its 1981 level. The important questions relate to whether economic growth can be sustained sufficiently long on current policies to bring unemployment down below one million.

Given that, with total unemployment of around 2.0 million, the current account is now (in 1989) in substantial deficit and inflation is rising, it is unlikely that unemployment will fall from its present level on current policies. This is mainly because current policies do nothing to address the **structural problems** that contribute to the poor performance of the UK economy in the medium and long term. In particular, the balance of payments equilibrium growth rate will need to be raised.

We are not optimistic about the future for two major reasons. Firstly, North Sea oil revenues are declining and will continue to decline. Nothing can be done about the deflation of this cushion, which up to now has helped to fill the growing gap between manufactured imports and exports, unless a dramatic rise in oil prices leads to further exploration and oil discoveries. Furthermore, it is unlikely that exports of services will grow sufficiently to fill the gap left by oil, let alone to offset the growing balance of trade deficit in manufactures. The second worry concerns the implications for British manufacturing industry of the movement towards the **single European market** in 1992.

1992 and All That

The plans for the creation of a single European market in 1992, in which all barriers to trade in goods and factors of production will disappear, is a major step along the way to complete European integration (and some would hope to a United States of Europe) which was started with the signing of the Treaty of Rome in 1957 and the creation of the European Economic Community (EEC). If past experience is anything to go by, however, the prospects for British industry look bleak. As an extract from the *Financial Times* remarks (see Figure 15), 'European industry is heading for a drastic and painful restructuring which will lead to the disappearance of many companies and could create higher unemployment in the next few years.'

EC integration 'threatens industry'

EUROPEAN industry is heading for a drastic and painful restructuring which will lead to the disappearance of many companies and could create higher unemployment in the next few years, several business leaders warned yesterday.

They expected these threatened upheavals to fuel pressures in the European Community for at least temporary trade protection against third countries, particularly Japan. EC governments could find such demands increasingly hard to resist.

The forecasts, made at a Financial Times conference in London, suggest that the recent euphoria generated by the EC's single market plan is start-

ing to dissipate as companies face fiercer competition.

Sir John Harvey-Jones, chairman of Parallax Enterprises and former chairman of ICI, said that in the next 10 years more than half of Europe's factories would be closed and half its companies would disappear or be absorbed by mergers.

He was optimistic that a more integrated European market would be achieved, but said: "We are going to see on our road to Nirvana degrees of pain which, if governments react as they normally do, they will seek to relieve through protection."

Mr Percy Barnevik, chairman of ABB, the recently merged Swedish-Swiss heavy engineering group, said it would not be easy for the EC simultaneously to restructure overcrowded sectors and to open its market to competition from Japan and South Korea.

There were 13 locomotive builders in Europe, compared with two in the US and three to four in Japan. A reduction was necessary to increase efficiency but would lead to higher unemployment, which would take time to absorb.

"These are the hard realities behind the nice words higher productivity and more competitive," he said. Political sensitivities would make restructuring even harder in Europe's poorer regions.

Mr Barnevik said that only a third of European companies would see themselves as winners from increased cross-border trade in a single market, while two-thirds would see themselves as losers.

Mr Robert Eaton, president of General Motors Europe, said severe cuts could be forced on European car makers if national restrictions on Japanese car imports were lifted.

The Japanese share of the European new car market could rise to as much as 30 per cent from the current 11 per cent, threatening about 10 big assembly plants and as many as 300,000 jobs in Europe. "It is not difficult to assume that it could be mainly the Japanese who will be the major beneficiaries of a unified single market," said Mr Eaton.

Though trade protection would only lull European industry into false complacency, it could become hard to resist, particularly if countries such as Japan and South Korea continued to promote their industries at the expense of their trading partners.

Figure 15 Article from the *Financial Times*, 23 November 1988

Britain remained outside the EEC until 1973. It then became a member on the pretext that access to a larger market would enable industry to reap economies of large-scale production and therefore enhance its competitiveness. More competition and less protection was to blow the cobwebs off British industry and enable it to compete more effectively in international markets. A government White Paper in 1970 entitled *Britain and the European Communities: An Economic Assessment* (Cmnd 4289) argued that there would be:

'. . . dynamic effects resulting from membership of a much larger and faster growing market. This would open up to our industrial producers substantial opportunities for increasing export sales, while at the same time exposing them more fully to the competition of European industries. No way has been found of quantifying these dynamic benefits, but if British industry responded vigorously to the stimuli, they would be considerable and highly advantageous. The acceleration of the rate of growth of industrial exports could then outpace any increase in the rate of growth of imports, with corresponding benefits to the balance of payments. Moreover, with such a response, the growth of industrial productivity would be accelerated as a result of increased competition and the advantages derived from specialization and larger scale production. This faster rate of growth would, in turn, accelerate the rate of growth of national production and real income.'

A further White Paper in 1971, *The United Kingdom and the European Communities* (Cmnd 4715), promised much of the same. The miserable economic performance of the British economy was compared with the vastly superior performance of the EEC, with the optimism expressed that:

'Her Majesty's Government is convinced that our economy [will be] stronger and our industries and peoples more prosperous if we join the European Communities than if we remain outside them. . . . Improvements in efficiency and competitive power should enable the UK to meet the balance of payments costs of entry over the next decade as they gradually build up. . . . [The] advantages will far outweigh the costs, provided we seize the opportunities of the far wider home market now open to us.'

The much-heralded beneficial winds of change turned into a gale of destruction for much of manufacturing industry, as might have been predicted from both economic theory and experience that when weak countries join **free-trade** areas or customs unions, the strong countries benefit at their expense. There is nothing in the doctrine of free trade that says that the **gains from trade** will be equally distributed among partners. Indeed, some countries may lose *absolutely* if the gains from specialization that free trade permits are offset by the unemployment of resources which comes about if import growth exceeds export growth, and the growth of output internally has to be constrained because of balance of payments difficulties. The doctrine of free trade ignores the balance of payments implications, implicitly assuming that the balance of payments looks after itself and that full employment is maintained.

There is precious little evidence that Britain joining the EEC has raised the underlying growth rate of the British economy consistent with balance of payments equilibrium. On the contrary, there is evidence that the budgetary costs of entry, the extent of import penetration from Europe, and a growing trade imbalance in manufactures, particularly with Germany, have tightened the balance of payments constraint on Britain's growth rate.

The year 1992 has now been set by the EEC for the complete liberalization of trade and the removal of all restrictions on the movement of capital and labour. The European Commission in Brussels is predicting substantial benefits, including a 4.5 per cent rise in GDP in the Community as a whole, a 6 per cent reduction in prices, and employment gains of 1.8 million (see the Cecchini Report, 1988); but it says nothing about the *distribution* of gains between member countries.

These further moves towards liberalization can only, in our view, strengthen the **centrifugal forces** already apparent within the Community by which the rich regions and countries get richer and the poor, poorer. 1992 does not augur well, therefore, for British industry, or for the British economy which is still chronically weak.

There can be no guarantee that the **mobility of factors of production**, such as labour and capital, between countries will equalize the rewards to factors of production, as orthodox (neoclassical) theory predicts, and that therefore per capita income levels will be equalized between countries. Orthodox theory says that factors of production migrate in response to differences in economic opportunity – and this is true – but the predictions of the theory seem to conflict with the facts. As labour migrates from a depressed to a more prosperous region or country, the supply of labour and unemployment is supposed to fall in the depressed region (with the demand for labour unchanged), so that wages rise, while in the more prosperous regions the increased supply of labour (with demand unchanged) is supposed to depress wages. Capital is supposed to 'migrate' the other way from prosperous regions where the wage rate is higher (and the rate of profit lower) to depressed regions where the wage rate is lower (and the rate of profit higher).

That is the neoclassical story, but it is a very static story which ignores the dynamic interactions between the supply and demand for factors of production as migration takes place. For example, as labour migration takes place it brings with it its own demands – in the form of demand for local goods, the provision of local services, housing and so on – so that the demand for labour increases with the supply of labour in the prosperous region, while in the depressed region from which the migrants come the demand is depressed. The equilibration of wages may not take place.

Likewise, as far as capital is concerned, the location of regional investment is not simply a function of relative wage rates, but also a function of productivity and the expected strength of demand. Therefore new investment is just as likely to flow to prosperous regions to which people are migrating as to depressed regions where the wages may be lower. Investment and employment growth tend to be complementary in the productive process.

All this is to say that initial differences in the level of development between regions and/or countries do not necessarily set up forces which eliminate those differences. On the contrary, forces are set up which may perpetuate and even widen these differences. The operation of these forces has been called by the Swedish economist, Gunnar Myrdal, the 'process of **circular and cumulative causation**'. These forces are factor mobility and free trade which lead to '**virtuous circles** of growth' in strong regions and countries and '**vicious circles** of poverty' in weak regions and countries. If the theory of circular and cumulative causation is correct, liberalization in 1992 will further widen regional/country disparities in levels of prosperity in Europe.

It must not be forgotten, too, that Britain is not only economically weak and relatively poor compared with many of its partners; it also lies on the *geographic periphery of Europe*. It is not in the 'centre' of the market for goods and services, but it is the 'centre' of a market that always exerts a strong gravitational pull. It is not an economic accident that the relatively depressed regions of the UK are on the geographic periphery of the UK or that many of the depressed regions of the EEC lie on the geographic periphery of Europe.

There is reason to be worried for the future, not only as a result of the effects of the operation of free-market forces pulling investment and skilled labour from Britain to the centre of Europe, but also because the Articles of Agreement of the EEC make it increasingly difficult for countries to pursue an independent economic policy, at least as far as the functioning of the real economy is concerned. It cannot offer incentives to industrial development because that means unfair competition; it cannot discriminate in favour of particular activities because that distorts competition; and it cannot restrict trade. Furthermore, if the idea of complete **monetary union** was adopted, with a European Central Bank and a **common currency**, countries would lose control over exchange rate policy and monetary policy as well. Britain in Europe would become like Scotland, or Wales, or any other region within the UK, or like the states within the USA; that is, completely at the mercy of market forces as far as economic performance is concerned, devoid of any instruments of economic policy, and with depressed regions dependent on the largesse of a central administration. This must be the worry for British industry, and therefore the British economy, in the 1990s.

KEY WORDS

Real economy	**Circular and cumulative causation**
Structural problems	**Virtuous and vicious circles**
Single European market	**Monetary union**
Free trade	**Common currency**
Gains from trade	
Centrifugal forces	
Mobility of factors of production	

Reading list

Aldcroft, D., 'Policy responses to industrial decline', *Economic Review*, vol. 5, May 1988.
Ball, Sir J., 'The UK economy: miracle or mirage?', *National Westminster Bank Quarterly Review*, Feb. 1989.
Cairncross, Sir A., 'Britain's industrial decline', *Royal Bank of Scotland Review*, Sept. 1988.
Cecchini, P., *The European Challenge 1992*, Wildwood House, 1988.

Essay topics

1. Why hasn't Britain's entry into the EEC in 1973 had any noticeable favourable effects on British economic performance?
2. Why may some countries lose at the expense of others within Customs Unions?
3. What is wrong with the argument that the free mobility of factors of production will tend to equalize the returns to factors of production between regions and countries?
4. What do you understand by the process of 'circular and cumulative causation'?
5. 'Having been bottom of the class, we have become more of an average performer.' (Sir J. Ball) What does this mean? Is it true?
6. At the start of Chapter 3 there is a quotation from a report of the House of Lords Select Committee on Overseas Trade. What is wrong with the climate? Why are oil measures important? What adverse effects threaten the standard of living?

Data Response Question 8

Your chance to provide a solution

This question is designed to allow you the opportunity to put your own interpretation on the facts as they have been presented in this book.

First of all read the **Postscript** that follows this chapter, and then attempt the following projects. Remember that you can agree or disagree with the author's *interpretation* of the facts.

1. Draft a critical letter to the Editor of *The Age*, either generally supporting the published article or offering alternative thoughts.
2. Prepare a short newspaper article, intended for a general readership, entitled 'Mrs Thatcher's economic miracle: fact or fiction?'

Postscript

'Economic historians will, I believe, look back with incredulity at this episode in British history.' A.P. Thirlwall

The article you are about to read appeared in *The Age* (an Australian daily newspaper) on 29 September 1988. It is based on a talk given by one of us (A.P.T.) during a visit to the University of Melbourne's Economics Department. The article was published under the title 'The myth of the Thatcher miracle'.

***

Since arriving in Australia two weeks ago for a brief academic visit, I keep hearing references to an alleged British economic miracle. There appears to be a widespread belief that nine years of Conservative government under Mrs Thatcher has resulted in a radical transformation of the British economy and a marked improvement in its potential for faster growth on a sustainable basis.

I am afraid to say that this is a myth. There has been no 'supply-side' revolution; the inertia and conservatism of British business, finance and other institutions remains, and the British economy is no closer to finding a solution to the simultaneous achievement of faster growth, full employment, stable prices and balance of payments equilibrium than it was before the 'Thatcher experiment' of monetarism, privatisation, trade union reform, tax reductions and rolling back the frontiers of the state.

What is being witnessed in Britain at the moment is a short-run unsustainable boom fuelled by consumption and this follows the deepest recession ever experienced in the British economy, which was deliberately engineered between 1979 and 1981 to curb the power of trade unions and to squeeze inflation out of the system. To argue my case, it is necessary to go back into history.

In the three decades following World War II, the British economy experienced the lowest rate of economic growth of any major industrialised country – averaging 2.5 per cent a year. Britain slipped from being one of the richest countries in the world to 19th in the per capita income stakes. The investment record was good by historical standards, but poor by international comparisons. The industrial relations record was generally appalling and the management of British industry weak.

The economy was perpetually plagued by balance of payments problems. The growth of export volume was the slowest of all OECD countries, while the country's appetite for foreign manufactured goods appeared insatiable. The effect of these adverse factors combined to produce deindustrialisation on a vast scale, with a loss of jobs in manufacturing industry of over three million between 1966 and 1979.

THE fatal policy mistake was to favor current consumption at the expense of investment and the foreign trade sector. In 1963, aware that living standards were falling relative to Europe, there was a dash for growth which precipitated the worst balance of payments crisis in history (till then) and contributed to the election of a Labor government in 1964.

The Labor administration put its faith in indicative planning and published a National Plan, setting a target growth rate of 4.5 per cent per annum. The need to deflate to tackle the balance of payments, however, made a nonsense of the plan, and it was soon abandoned.

The Pavlovian response was to look to the Common Market (EEC) for salvation. The predictions of economic theory that within customs unions the weak get weaker and the strong get stronger were ignored. Britain joined the EEC in 1973 and some of the worst fears of the critics of entry have materialised.

The trade deficit in manufactured goods, particularly with Germany, has risen by alarming proportions, and in many spheres of economic life it is now no longer possible to pursue an independent economic policy.

In the late 1960s the spectre of inflation began to rear its ugly head. This was fuelled by sterling devaluation in 1967 and aggressive trade union behavior, and later exacerbated by the commodity price boom of the early 1970s.

Neither the Conservatives between 1970 and 1974 nor the Labor Party between 1974 and 1979 were able to slay the dragon. The trade unions will still not admit that wage inflation is a major source of price inflation (independent of prior increases in the money supply), and the Labor Party – a prisoner of the trade unions – will still not publicly advocate incomes policy.

It was largely the irresponsible behavior of the trade unions, and the serious inflation of the late 1970s, that brought Mrs Thatcher to power in 1979.

The 'Iron Lady' came into office determined to reduce the role of the state in economic affairs; to end all forms of corporatism, and to weaken the power of the trade unions on the assumption that excessive government intervention and the power of the unions have been the major sources of Britain's long-term economic malaise.

So, the vital question remains, has nine years of Thatcherism made any difference?

THE first three years of Mrs Thatcher's reign turned out to be an economic nightmare. Notwithstanding the cushion of North Sea oil, the Government managed to engineer the biggest recession in recorded history – worse than the great depression of the 1930s. Between 1979 and 1981 total output fell by three per cent and unemployment rose from one million to 2.5 million.

Monetary and fiscal policy was exceedingly tight, and the effective exchange rate rose by over 20 per cent which also contributed to the recession.

As justification, it is sometimes argued that a cathartic exercise was necessary on the assumption that leaner means fitter, and out of the ashes some phoenix would rise. For much of British industry, however, leaner meant not fitter but strangulation and even death. Manufacturing output has only now reached again its 1979 level.

This economic masochism coincided with annual flows of tax revenue and foreign exchange from North Sea oil of close to £10 billion, for which the British economy has nothing to show. The revenue was frittered away in dole payments and expenditure on foreign imports. Economic historians will, I believe, look back with incredulity at this episode in British economic history.

Since 1982 there has been a general recovery of output and employment, and currently the economy is growing at close to four per cent a year. The Government and press proclaim an economic miracle, justifying the earlier sacrifice. I view the situation as more like someone having deliberately thrown themselves off a cliff and then congratulating themselves at having nearly climbed back to the top.

For the fact is that if the Thatcher years are taken as a whole, the average annual growth of GDP is only two per cent, investment is only recently back to its 1979 level; unemployment is still more than double what it was in 1979, and the country is heading for a huge balance of payments crisis like days of old.

The major achievement has been the control of inflation through the crude weapon of unemployment. The reduction of inflation had nothing directly to do with the pursuit of monetarist policies, since the chosen nominal money supply target (M3) proved to be uncontrollable. But even with unemployment at over two million, the inflation rate is starting to rise again.

Likewise, there have been some welcome trade union reforms, and

Table 15 Macroeconomic indicators by political regimes

	Growth of GDP (%)	*Inflation Rate* (%)	*Unemployment Percentage*
		(Annual Averages)	
Conservatives 1951–1964	3.2	3.5	1.7
Labour 1964–1970	2.4	5.2	2.0
Conservatives 1970–1974	2.4	11.7	3.1
Labour 1974–1979	1.8	21.2	4.7
Conservatives 1979–1988	2.0	8.4	9.5

the number of strikes has fallen dramatically, but this is also largely a function of the high levels of unemployment.

State industries and public corporations have been sold off at a handsome profit to speculators, but the management of the enterprises remains exactly the same.

Tax rates have been reduced, particularly for the better off, but no economic research can find any evidence that this makes any significant difference to work effort. The price has been a deterioration in many of the public services. The division between rich and poor has widened, as has the geographic divide between the depressed north of the country and the more affluent south.

BRITAIN'S Achilles heel is still its balance of payments, but the Government shows no sign of appreciating either the nature or magnitude of the problem. The forecast deficit on current account for 1988 is now £15 billion, four times greater than the deficit forecast in the April budget.

The British economic miracle is a mirage, but brilliantly propagandised by the media.

Index